Faces of Government

Mary Cairo & Luci Soncin

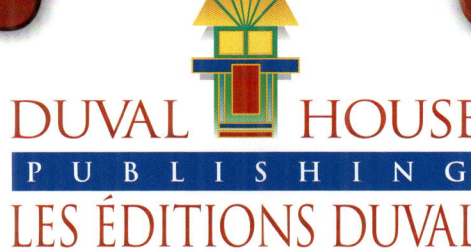

DUVAL HOUSE PUBLISHING
Les Éditions Duval

Copyright © 2003 Duval House Publishing Inc.

All rights reserved. No part of this work covered by the copyrights hereon may be reproduced or used in any form or by any means—graphic, electronic, electrostatic, or mechanical—without the prior written permission of the publisher, or in case of photocopying or other reprographic copying, a licence from Access Copyright (The Canadian Copyright Licensing Agency) 1 Yonge Street, Suite 1900, Toronto, Ontario M5E 1E5, Fax (416) 868-1261. This applies to classroom usage as well.

5 4 3 2 1

Printed and bound in Canada

Duval House Publishing Inc.
18228 – 102 Avenue
Edmonton, Alberta T5S 1S7
Ph: 1-800-267-6187
Fax: (780) 482-7213
Website: http://www.duvalhouse.com

Authors
Mary Cairo
Luci Soncin

National Library of Canada Cataloguing in Publication

Cairo, Mary
   Faces of government / Mary Cairo, Luci Soncin.

Includes index.
For use in grade 5.
ISBN 1-55220-464-2

   1. Federal government--Textbooks. 2. Elections--Textbooks. 3. Citizenship--Textbooks. I. Soncin, Luciana II. Title.

JL75.C19 2003   321.02   C2003-905234-6

Project Team
Project Manager: Karen Iversen
Editors: Betty Gibbs, Karen Iversen, Lynn Hamilton, Shauna Babiuk
Cover and text design: Claudia Pompei, Obsidian Multimedia
Photo research: David Strand
Production: Claudia Pompei, Leslie Stewart, Jeff Miles
Illustrations and maps: Claudia Pompei; Johnson Cartographics Inc., Wendy Johnson; Mitch Fortier
Photographer: New Visions Photography, Brad Callihoo
Photo Shoot Coordinator: Roberta Wildgoose
Photographic Models: Shimona DaCosta-Alexis, Elisa Lee, Lindsey MacLean, Raymond Mahava

Manufacturers
Screaming Colour, Inc., Friesens

Validators
Educational
Mary Bender, Program Consultant
Waterloo Catholic District School Board

Robert Mewhinney, Instructional Leader
Toronto District School Board

Marian Reich, Teacher
Muirhead Public School
Toronto District School Board

Audrey M. Sgroi, Teacher
Toronto Catholic District School Board

Theresa Smith, Teacher
St. Gerald Catholic Elementary School
Toronto Catholic District School Board

Kim Wallace, Coordinator of Social, Canadian and World Studies
Halton District School Board

Bias Reviewer
Kennard Ramphal, Teacher
Toronto District School Board

Content
Dr. Jeffrey Keshen, Associate Professor
History Department
University of Ottawa

Aboriginal Content
Brenda Davis, Educator (Retired)
Six Nations of Grand River

Acknowledgements

The authors would like to express their sincere thanks and appreciation to the many people who contributed to the creation of this book. We are grateful for the invaluable guidance and cheerful support that Karen Iversen has patiently provided to us throughout this project. Our sincerest thanks go to Betty Gibbs for providing us with insightful comments, creative suggestions, and of course, her editorial expertise. We appreciate the efforts of David Strand to locate photographs and images that visually bring the concept of government to life, as well as Claudia Pompei's skillful, artistic designs that clarify and enhance the text the students will read. The authors appreciate the information and contributions that many others provided in their areas of expertise, in particular, Mr. Justice (Honourable) Frank Iacobucci, Michelle Astill, and Rebecca Palladina.

We would like to thank our families for their words of encouragement and the quiet support they offered throughout the various stages of this project. Particular thanks go to Cassandra, Jonathan, Vanessa, and John Paul for showing us one facet of their community government in action.

We acknowledge the financial support of the Government of Canada through the Book Publishing Industry Development Program (BPIDP) for our publishing activities.

Many website addresses have been identified in this textbook. These are provided as suggestions and are not intended to be a complete resource list. Duval House Publishing does not guarantee that these websites will not change or will continue to exist. Duval House does not endorse the content of the website nor any websites linked to the site. Students should consult with their teacher whenever using Internet resources.

Credits

Every effort has been made to correctly identify and credit all sources. The publisher would appreciate notification of any omissions or errors so that they may be corrected. All images are copyright © of their respective copyright holders, as listed below. Reproduced with permission.

Abbreviations

(cw) = clockwise (t) = top (r) = right (l) = left (b) = bottom (m) = middle; ADLPSC = *A Day in the Life of the Public Service of Canada*; CIC = Citizenship and Immigration Canada; DCH = Department of Canadian Heritage; DoD = Department of Defense (US); EC = Elections Canada; HoC = House of Commons; LP/BP = Library of Parliament / Bibliothèque du Parlement; NAC = National Archives of Canada; PWGSC = Public Works and Government Services Canada; RCMP = Royal Canadian Mounted Police; SCC = Supreme Court of Canada; SGG = Secretary to the Governor General; VC = Volunteer Canada

front cover Adrienne Clarkson, see p. 65 (tr); Paul Okalik, see p. 44 (m); ceremony, © Canadian Museum of Civilization, photographer Tom Afoldi, image no. AC2000-139-8; Jean Augustine, HoC photographer Chris Diotte **back cover** Pierre Pettigrew, see p. 68 (b); Thelma Chalifoux, see p. 84 (b); Samantha Moonsammy, see p. 26 (b) **2** (tl) Photo courtesy The Right Honourable Kim Campbell (by Zack Allen) (tr) Jean Charest, Premier of Quebec (br) Sgt. Joanne Stoeckl **3** (tl) HoC photographer Chris Diotte (mr) EC **4** (national flag) Source: DCH. Reproduced with the permission of the Minister of PWGSC, 2003 **5** (cw from tr) Richard T. Nowitz/CORBIS/ Magmaphoto.com; Copyright VC; City of Windsor; no credit; CIC; SGG; Courtesy of the Department of National Defence, Photo by Cpl Jolin; EC **6** (quote) Pearson, Lester B. *Notes from the Prime Minister's remarks at the opening of Expo 67 in Montreal.* Ottawa: Office of the Prime Minister, 1967. Source: The National Library of Canada's website www.nlc-bnc.gc.ca. Copyright Her Majesty the Queen in Right of Canada. Reproduced courtesy of the Privy Council Office (cw from tr) NAC; NAC; Courtesy of the DCH; Corel 454062 **7** (all but br) Courtesy of the DCH (br) Courtesy of the Government of Canada **8** "vote for me" sign, EC **10** (t) DoD photo by Helene C. Stikkel, 981013-D-2987S-196 (b) © Copyright The British Museum **11** Toronto Community News: *The Mirror and The Guardian*, http://www.insidetoronto.ca/to/ **12** (t) AFP/CORBIS/Magmaphoto.com (b) see p. 10 (t) **13** (t) AFP/CORBIS/ Magmaphoto.com (b) Office of the Prime Minister of New Zealand **14** (b) CP/Andrew Vaughan **18** (t) Copyright VC (b) © Royalty-Free CORBIS/ Magmaphoto.com **19** (t) © Canada Post Corporation, 1947. Reproduced with permission (b) CIC **20** (Pope) Bill Wittman **21** (t) CP/Ron Poling (m) Source of Charter: DCH–Human Rights Program. Reproduced with the permission of the Minister of PWGSC, 2003 (b) © SCC, photo by Philippe Landreville **22** (cw from tl) © Royalty-Free/CORBIS/Magmaphoto.com; EC; Source: Translation Bureau, an Agency of PWGSC. Reproduced with the permission of the Minister of PWGSC, 2003; Courtesy of Public Affairs Branch, Canada Customs and Revenue Agency **23** (ml) Photo courtesy of Canada Post (b) Courtesy of Peel District School Board - Media Technology, photo by Neil Kotch and Dave McNee (poem) "I'm a Canadian," poem by Ashlee Clarke. Source: provided by Canadianculture.com **24** (tm) CIDA Photo: Roger LeMoyne (br) CIDA Photo: David Barbour **26** (all but b) Copyright VC (b) Aaron Deane (poem) by Anne Brandt. Duval House Publishing was unable to locate Anne Brandt, and would appreciate any further information on this poem. **30** (t) CIC (b) Jim Wilkes/Toronto Star **31** (bl) www.painetworks.com, photo by Craig Lovell (statistics) Source: *Facts and Figures 2001: Immigration Overview,* from the CIC website, www.cic.gc.ca/english/pub/facts2001/1imm-05.html. Adapted with the permission of the Minister of PWGSC, 2003 **33** (all r) CIC **36** (statistics) Source: Table G2, "Immigration by Calendar Year, 1852-1996" *Citizenship and Immigration Statistics 1996,* a publication of CIC, from www.cic.gc.ca/english/pdf/pub/ 1996stats.pdf. Adapted with the permission of the Minister of PWGSC, 2003 **37** (b) CIC (statistics) Source: Table 1, "Persons granted Canadian citizenship by fiscal year, 1919-20 to 1951-52 and by calendar year, 1952 to 1996." From publication cited on p. 36 **38, 39** (all) © Canadian Museum of Civilization, photographer Tom Afoldi, image numbers (from p. 38 (l)) AC2000-139-16; AC2000-139-24; AC2000-139-11; AC2000-139-8; AC2000-139-26 (oath) CIC **41** (t) Coin design courtesy of the Royal Canadian Mint / Image de la pièce courtoisie de la Monnaie royale canadienne (r) Corel 462071 (l) Tourism Toronto **44** (t) Corel 462091 (m) PATRICIA D'SOUZA/ NUNATSIAQ NEWS (b) Corporation of the City of Mississauga, Mayor's Office **46** (mr) Courtesy Office of the Mayor of Toronto **49** (t) *The Minden Times,* Minden, Ontario (b) Sandra Bussin, City Councillor **50** (tl) Courtesy Kelvin Scheuer (b) City of Windsor **52** (bl) Corel 462091 (br) Tessa Macintosh **53** (t) Courtesy of the Office of the Lieutenant Governor of Ontario (m) Photo courtesy of Peel District School Board - Media Technology, photo by Neil Kotch and Dave McNee (b) Cattroll Photo **55** (t) Reproduced with the permission of Dr. Kuldip Kular (m) New Democratic Party of Ontario (b) Ernie Eves election sign, ©2003 The Ontario PC Party **56** (t) Russell Diabo (all but t) Cattroll Photo **57** (t l and r) Cattroll Photo (m) Government of Nunavut (b) CP/Shaun Best **58** (all) Photos by Rebecca Palladina **59** (material from and about Ms. Norwegian) Bernadette Norwegian, Intergovernmental Affairs Specialist with the Department of Indian Affairs and Northern Development, quote and photograph from "ADLPSC" © Treasury Board of Canada Secretariat, 1999. Reproduced with the permission of the President of Treasury of Canada Secretariat (b) Peter Power/Toronto Star **62** (t) Sgt. Joanne Stoeckl (m) Diana Murphy (b) Photo courtesy The Right Honourable Kim Campbell (by Zack Allen) **63** Reproduction authorized by the LP / Reproduction autorisée par la BP, Mone's Photography **65** (all but tr) Sgt. Joanne Stoeckl (tr) SGG **66** (all) SGG **67** (all) SGG **68** (all but b) Diana Murphy (b) Courtesy Office of Minister for International Trade **71** (material from and about Dr. Cosens) Dr. Sue Cosens, Whale Researcher with the Department of Fisheries and Oceans, quote and photograph from "ADLPSC"; (material from and about Ms. Vansickle) Tracey Vansickle, Foreign Service Officer with CIC, quote and photograph from "ADLPSC"; (material from and about Mr. Peers) Glen Peers, Park Warden with Parks Canada, quote and photograph from "ADLPSC" (all material) © Treasury Board of Canada Secretariat, 1999. Reproduced with the permission of the President of Treasury of Canada Secretariat **72** (t, bl) RCMP-GRC (br) Richard T. Nowitz/CORBIS/ Magmaphoto.com **73** (material from and about Mr. Polegato) Dan Polegato, Farrier with the RCMP Musical Ride, quote and photograph from "ADLPSC" © Treasury Board of Canada Secretariat, 2000. Reproduced with the permission of the President of Treasury of Canada Secretariat (b) Corel 454014 **74** (t) Source: Department of Foreign Affairs and International Trade, reproduced with the permission of the Minister of PWGSC, 2003 (b) Joshua Berson Photography **76** (from t to b) Reproduction authorized by the LP/Reproduction autorisée par la BP, Stephen Fenn; Illusions Photographic/Calgary, AB; HoC photographer Chris Diotte; © SCC, photo by Larry Munn **77** (l) HoC of Canada **78** Reproduction authorized by the LP / Reproduction autorisée par la BP, Stephen Fenn **79** (all) Reproduction authorized by the LP / Reproduction autorisée par la BP, Mone's Photography **80** (b) House of Commons photographer **82** (all) Courtesy Peter Adams **84** (t) Malak, Ottawa (b) Courtesy Office of the Honourable Senator Thelma Chalifoux **86** © SCC, photo by Philippe Landreville **87** (t) © SCC, photo by Larry Munn **90** (t) Courtesy Tree Canada Foundation (m) AP/Wide World Photos (b) ©Reuters NewMedia Inc./CORBIS/Magmaphoto.com **91** (t) Courtesy of the Department of National Defence, Photo by Cpl Jolin (m and b) Winnipeg Free Press, *A Red Sea Rising: The Flood of the Century,* reproduced with permission **95** (t) Reproduced with the permission of the International Olympic Committee (b) Courtesy Tree Canada Foundation **98** (t) Reproduction authorized by the LP / Reproduction autorisée par la BP, Stephen Fenn **99** (t) ©NCC/CCN (mr) see p. 4 (ml) Corel 454010 (b) Courtesy of Pat Huck **100, 101** Beverly Ann Robertson **102** (t, bl) Malak, Ottawa (br) Reproduction authorized by the LP / Reproduction autorisée par la BP, Mone's Photography **103** (t) NAC/C-008007 (m) Yousuf Karsh/NAC/C-021557 (b) Courtesy of the Weyburn Review **104** (t, m) Reproduction authorized by the LP / Reproduction autorisée par la BP: (t) Stephen Fenn: (m) Gordon King (bl) NAC/C-018713/G. Horne Russell (br) Courtesy of the Hon. Charlie Watt **105** (t) Reproduction authorized by the LP / Reproduction autorisée par la BP, W.J.L. Gibbons (bl) Malak, Ottawa (br) (material from and about Mr. Brisebois) Michel Brisebois, Rare Book Curator with the National Library of Canada, quote and photograph from "ADLPSC" © Treasury Board of Canada Secretariat, 1999. Reproduced with the permission of the President of Treasury of Canada Secretariat **106** (tl, bl) Reproduction authorized by the LP / Reproduction autorisée par la BP: (tl) Tom Littlemore: (bl) Mone's Photography (tm) Source: Department of Foreign Affairs and International Trade, reproduced with the permission of the Minister of PWGSC, 2003 (tr) Duncan Cameron/NAC/PA-114544 (br) Courtesy Veterans Affairs Canada **107** (all) Malak, Ottawa **108** (t) © Lee Snider/CORBIS/Magmaphoto.com (m) Reproduction authorized by the LP / Reproduction autorisée par la BP, Mone's Photography (b) PWGSC, "Photograph of the Office of George Étienne Cartier," © Parliament Hill. Reproduced with the permission of the Minister of PWGSC, 2003 **109** (t) Notman & Son/NAC/C-002090 (b) Glenbow Archives NA-404-1 **110** (all but l) Courtesy of Stan Milosevic (l) PWGSC. "Photograph of the Confederation Room," © Parliament Hill. Reproduced with the permission of the Minister of PWGSC, 2003 **111** Courtesy of the DCH. Reproduced with permission **112** (all) © SCC, photos by Philippe Landreville **114** (all but b) SGG (b) Jean-Marc Carisse **115** (tl) SGG (tr) Gar Lunney/National Film Board of Canada. Photothèque/NAC/PA-144172 (b, l to r) William James Topley/NAC/PA-025686; Doug MacLellan/Hockey Hall of Fame; photo courtesy of John Sokolowski; NAC/ C-017372 **116** (tm, tr) see p. 79 (all); (ml) see p. 4 (national flag); (mr) see p. 111; (bl) see p. 112 (all); (bm) see p. 115 (tl) **118** (all but b) EC (b) Eleanor Milne and Chris Fairbrother, detail from *The Vote* 1979-1980, Indiana limestone, 121.9 x 182.8 cm; HoC, Ottawa, reproduced with permission of the Government of Canada **119** (b) Photo by John Rennison, The Hamilton Spectator **120** (from t) Courtesy of Canada's NDP; Denis Drever; Courtesy of the Bloc Québécois; Courtesy of the Canadian Alliance; Reproduced with the permission of the Federal Liberal Agency of Canada; Courtesy of the New Democratic Party of Canada; Courtesy of the PC Party of Canada **121** (t) Photo by Jacques Pontbrilland (b) CP/Daily Gleaner/Diane Doiron **123** (t) CP/Fred Chartrand (m) www.painetworks.com, photo by Bill Bachmann (b) CP/Tannis Toohey **125** (all) EC **127** (t) HoC/Ottawa, ON **130** "vote for me" sign, ballot box, and screen provided by EC

To the Student

Three levels of government in Canada—municipal (local), provincial or territorial, and federal—enable communities, provinces and territories, and the country to work together to fulfil citizens' needs and goals. These governments work with citizens and communities across Canada to organize their efforts and contributions and to share Canada's resources.

Government in Canada affects the everyday lives of everyone. For instance, it sets guidelines for what can be shown on television. It determines what you will study in school. Your government works to ensure that playgrounds, parks, beaches, and ski hills are available for you to enjoy. Government is especially visible during national celebrations, elections, and crisis situations. People often discuss and debate the ways that government decisions are affecting their lives.

You will encounter many "faces of government" throughout the textbook. They include government leaders and workers, volunteers, and other citizens. Many of them share their ideas about government and discuss their roles in Canada's government.

You might be wondering how someone who is 10 or 11 years old can be a part of Canada's government system. Even though Canadians are not eligible to vote until they are 18, youth can become knowledgeable about Canada and its system of government now. You can learn about ways that Canadian citizens of all ages participate in government.

This textbook is designed to help you learn more about government in Canada. Throughout the book, four Canadian children invite you to practise some of the skills needed to participate in and contribute to Canada. By doing so, you take the challenge of becoming an active citizen and learn that one of the important faces of government in Canada is YOU!

Contents

Overview	Faces of Government	2
Chapter 1	Types of Government	10
Chapter 2	Being a Citizen	18
Chapter 3	Becoming a Citizen	30
Chapter 4	Levels of Government	44
Chapter 5	Federal Government: Executive Branch	62
Chapter 6	Federal Government: Legislative and Judicial Branches	76
Chapter 7	Interactions Among Levels of Government	90
Chapter 8	Structures and Symbols	98
Chapter 9	Federal Elections	118

Finishing Touches 132

Glossary 134

Index 137

Overview
Faces of Government

" In a democracy, government isn't something that a small group of people do to everybody else, it's not even something they do for everybody else, it should be something they do *with* everybody else."

– *Kim Campbell, former Prime Minister*

" Today, Quebecers gave the Liberal Party of Quebec a government in the service of its citizens."

– *Jean Charest, Premier of Quebec*

" Citizenship is about taking an active part in learning what is happening in government so you can use your vote wisely."

– *Andrew Newlin, Winnipeg, Manitoba*

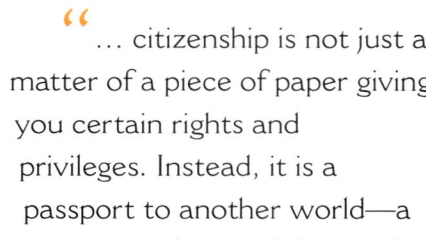

" … citizenship is not just a matter of a piece of paper giving you certain rights and privileges. Instead, it is a passport to another world—a world where you can understand the needs of others, where you can reach out and be part of something larger than yourself, your family, or your original community."

– *Adrienne Clarkson, Governor General*

"When you take an interest in your community, when you form an opinion in politics, and when you cast your vote, you are part of government."

– *Jean Augustine, Secretary of State for Multiculturalism and Status of Women*

"Parliament Hill is one of the most recognized Canadian symbols. The Peace Tower, the Eternal Flame, and the Canadian flag with its maple leaf are what Canadians are all about."

– *Tana Godbout, tour guide, Ottawa, Ontario*

"The right to vote is the very basis of our system."

– *Jean-Pierre Kingsley, Chief Electoral Officer of Canada*

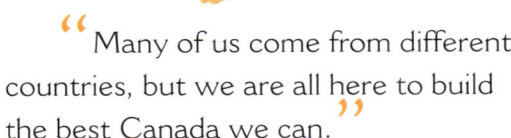

"Many of us come from different countries, but we are all here to build the best Canada we can."

– *Shellina Gupta, Sarnia, Ontario*

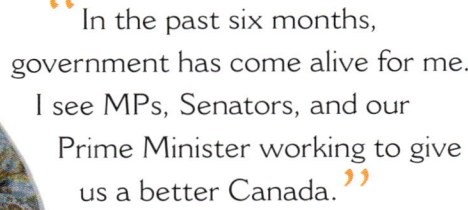

"In the past six months, government has come alive for me. I see MPs, Senators, and our Prime Minister working to give us a better Canada."

– *Tony Rimko, parliamentary page, Ottawa, Ontario*

Do Discuss Discover

1. In your notebook, write a question about any of the statements you do not understand.
2. Re-write each of the statements you do understand in your own words.

Group Needs

Everyone has individual needs that must be met. Our basic physical needs are for food and shelter. People also have social needs, such as the need to be loved and to feel they belong in a group.

Groups of people also have needs. They need to have organization, leadership, security, rules, and laws. Group needs must be met so that people can live together safely and happily.

At school you are often asked to work in a small group. In order to complete your task, your group must agree on some rules that the members will follow. Rules are also important for the whole class so people can get along and work together. For example, a rule that only one person speaks at a time allows everyone to hear each other's good ideas.

Each classroom is also part of the larger group called the school, and the school is part of a community.

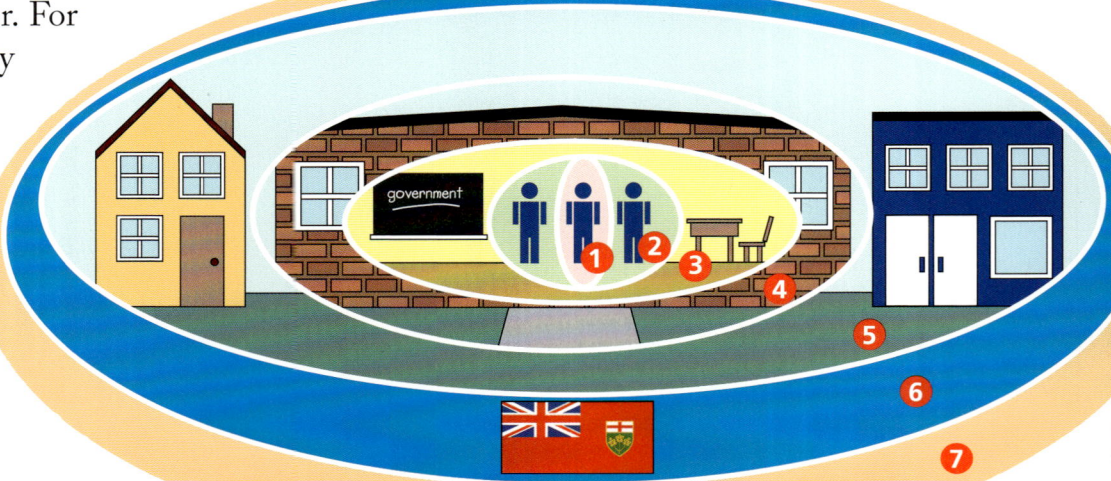

❶ Individual
❷ Small group
❸ Classroom
❹ School
❺ Community
❻ Province/Territory
❼ Country

Groups and Governments

Citizens are people who live in a community, province or territory, and country. Citizens choose leaders and representatives to listen to their ideas and make decisions on their behalf. A group of people who provide leadership and organization, make decisions and laws, and enforce the laws is a **government**. Governments serve the group needs of all citizens.

Laws protect the **rights** of individuals. Rights are privileges or freedoms that citizens are entitled to or can expect. They are passed as law by a government for the good of its citizens. Laws also state citizens' **responsibilities**. These are duties that are expected of citizens to make sure everyone's rights are respected and needs are met.

Government and Citizens in Action

Citizens contribute to their communities and fulfil their responsibilities in many ways. Some people volunteer their time and energy. Citizens also contribute by choosing people to represent them in government. In turn, the government is responsible for meeting citizens' needs and protecting their rights.

Do Discuss Discover

1. a) On a sheet of paper in your notebook, write today's date and the title Government and Citizens in Action. Put the numbers 1 to 8 down the left side of the page, leaving two lines after each number.

   b) Draw a line dividing the page into two columns and add the headings What I Think and What I Found Out.

   c) Look at the photographs on this page. Beside each number in your notes, write one statement about what you think that numbered photograph is showing about Canada's government or its citizens. At the end of this study, you will return to this activity and add to or change the statements you wrote.

A World Exposition

A **World Exposition** is a huge world fair where many countries display and demonstrate special things that their citizens have done. People around the world are invited to see displays of inventions and innovations that could benefit everyone in the world. Expositions have showcased advances in medical research, science, education, and many other fields.

Every few years, a different country hosts a World Exposition. Participating countries build structures called **pavilions** on the exposition site to hold displays and exhibits that relate to the theme of the exposition.

Canada hosted Expo '67 in Montreal and Expo '86 in Vancouver.

The Canada pavilion at Expo '67 in Montreal.

" Today we pay our tribute to the dedication and the effort of many men and women who have made all this possible. Montreal has proven its capacity to carry through such an undertaking and its Mayor has shown the inspired and dynamic leadership which was essential.

" So have the people of Canada as a whole, through the cooperation of the three levels of government that was required."

– *former Prime Minister Lester B. Pearson at the opening of Expo '67, Montreal, April 27, 1967*

Lester B. Pearson is surrounded by Canadian political leaders on the opening day of Expo '67 in Montreal.

The Canada pavilion at Expo '86 in Vancouver.

The Canada pavilion at the World Exposition in Seville, Spain, in 1992.

The Canada pavilion at the World Exposition in Hanover, Germany, in 2000.

The Canada pavilion at the World Exposition in Lisbon, Portugal, in 1998.

The World Exposition Proposal

As you learn about government in Canada, your teacher may put you in groups of four or five and assign you one or more parts of this special project.

Each group will select a city in Ontario and create a proposal to demonstrate their ideas for the upcoming World Exposition. Your goal is to convince the selection authorities to choose your location as the host for the next World Exposition. Below is a summary of the parts of the proposal.

- Decide upon a theme that is important to Canadians. It will be the theme of your exposition.
- Identify and advertise the many attractions that your city has to offer.
- Do research about people involved in Canada's government system.
- Identify the many needs your city will have as it hosts events and visitors from around the world; identify the roles of the three levels of government.
- Create a model and/or a diorama of your proposed Canada pavilion.
- Share your proposal with others at a display presentation.

> Ottawa is considering making a proposal to host the 2007/2008 World Exposition that would focus on living in our changing environment. This would coincide with the 150th anniversary of the founding of Ottawa.

The Canada pavilion at the World Exposition in Taejon, South Korea, in 1993.

Active Involvement

As you learn about the government and citizens of Canada, you will take part in a variety of projects. Your teacher may assign you one or more parts of the World Exposition Proposal described on page 7 and/or projects listed on this page. These are different ways of thinking and learning about our type of government.

Scrapbook

Throughout this unit, you will work on collecting information about the government at work from sources such as newspaper and magazine articles, the Internet, and pictures. You will read, reflect on, and summarize the focus of each chapter. You will also include one sample of your work for each chapter.

Model of a Government Building

Chapter 8 concentrates on symbols of Canada and the structures that house Canada's government. In groups, you will create a model of one of the key government buildings. This will give you an opportunity to build and decorate a structure.

Election Simulation

The election process is a central part of our type of government. In Chapter 9, you will participate as a class in a simulation of an election to learn about the election process and the contributions of different people who are involved. This highlights the importance of the right to vote in a free election and the responsibility of making an informed decision.

Do Discuss Discover

1. As a class, start building a display of words that are the foundation for understanding government. This wall design is one type of graphic organizer you can use. Add new words from each chapter to your classroom organizer as you learn them.

Creating a Class Canadian Flag

Your class will need
- 1 rectangle of white felt fabric for the flag base (130 cm x 60 cm)
- 2 rectangles of red felt fabric for the red flag panels (33 cm x 60 cm each)
- 1 square of red felt fabric for a maple leaf (60 cm x 60 cm)
- fabric glue or glue gun
- coloured fabric markers

You will need
- 1 sheet of red construction paper
- pencil, pen
- scissors
- photograph of yourself that will not be returned

Your teacher will cut a maple leaf from the square of red felt. You should follow the steps below:

1. Trace two left hands and two right hands on a sheet of red construction paper.
2. On each of the two left hands, write a one-sentence response to the question "Who am I?" Responses may include descriptions of yourself, your heritage, personality traits, hobbies, activities, or talents, or something that is important to you.
3. On each of the two right hands, write a one-sentence response to "What is Canada?" Responses may include geographic features, personalities, customs, or groups.
4. Cut out your four hands. Curl up the fingers and glue them on the red felt panels. The curling fingers can interlock with other students' hands.
5. With the teacher's help, glue your photograph in the centre area of the maple leaf with the other class members' photographs. Next, mount the red felt panels and maple leaf on the white felt rectangle.
6. Use a fabric marker to sign your name in the white area surrounding the maple leaf.
7. Display the flag in your classroom.

Chapter 1
Types of Government

There are several different kinds of government in the world. Canada's government is a **democracy**. Its government members are elected by the people to represent them and make decisions and laws for them.

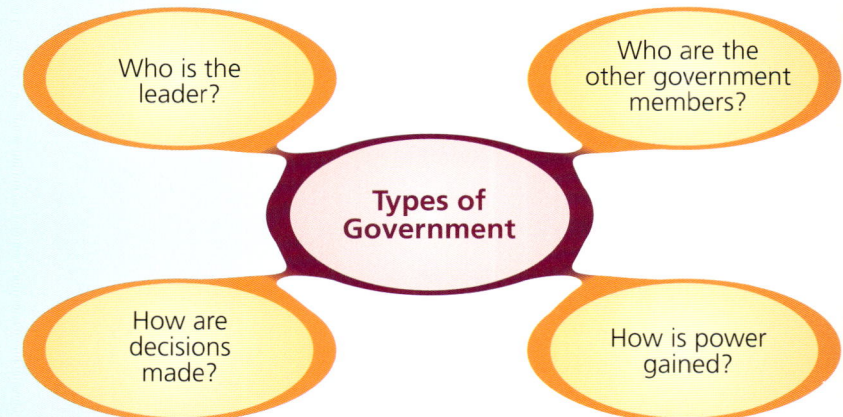

" In a democracy, we have the right to run for political office, belong to the political party of our choice, and help choose our government representatives. "

– *Marla Gates, Summerside, Prince Edward Island*

Focus on Learning

In this chapter, you will learn about
- getting information from quotations
- different types of government
- types of democracy

Vocabulary
- democracy
- monarchy
- parliament
- dictatorship
- consensus

" Here each individual is interested not only in his own affairs, but in the affairs of the state as well .... a man who has no interest in politics ... has no business here at all.

" I was a leader of government in Athens for 30 years. I worked hard to improve life in Athens for all citizens. If everyone is involved in trying to make a better life for the whole community, then it will be a better place for all. "

– *Pericles of Athens, c.450 BCE*

Getting Information from Quotations

Newspaper and magazine articles, books, interviews, films and videos, speeches, letters, photographs, and diaries are all sources of research information. Reviewing past newspaper articles is one way to gather historical information. Watching and listening to daily newscasts allows you to follow recent events.

Often a news reporter includes statements made by someone who witnessed or participated in an event. When a person's exact words are reported, it is called a **direct quotation**. When a direct quotation is written down, the words have quotation marks around them.

Sometimes a news reporter uses his or her own words to tell readers what a person said. This is called **reported speech**. Reported speech does not have quotation marks.

If direct quotations and reported speech are accurately presented, they can provide reliable and interesting first-hand details about an event. To get information from quotations, ask yourself the following questions:

- What was the event or occasion?
- Who is making the statement?
- Is it a direct quotation or reported speech, or is there a combination of both?
- Is the person's statement fact or opinion?
- How can you be sure that the person's opinion is based on fact? For example, is the person an authority about the subject? Are there facts to support the opinion?

2003 Mayoral Race

Tory brings election kickoff to North York

On Wednesday, John Tory began his campaign for mayor of Toronto to a crowd of 300. He told the crowd that, in order to be great, Toronto needs new leadership and new ideas. "We are only going to make the city work better if we decide to manage better."

"It seems to be difficult to focus on top priorities for the future and getting some things done, because there are so many items of unfinished business," said Tory. He promises that as mayor he would be committed to making sure that help is given where it is needed.

– *The Mirror*, March 28, 2003

1. Use the questions above to read and understand the article on the right.
2. Re-read the quotation by Pericles on page 10. What do you think is his message to people? Write your thoughts in your notebook.
3. Discuss with a partner how quotations can be used as a source of information.

Types of Government

There are three basic types of government. They differ in who has power and how decisions are made. Some governments are chosen by the citizens. In other governments, most of the citizens have no say in how members of the government are chosen or how the laws are made.

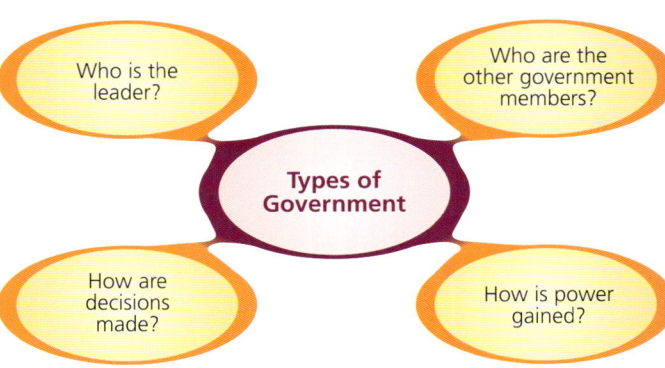

Monarchy

In a **monarchy**, a king, queen, or emperor inherits the position of government leader. This means that when a monarch dies, his or her son, daughter, or nearest relative takes over. In the past, monarchs made laws and decisions based on whatever they thought was proper.

In Saudi Arabia, the monarch is the chief of state and government leader. The king chooses a number of advisors, which includes many family members. Sometimes the advisors take part in special public sessions. Citizens can approach the advisors to ask for help, make complaints, and suggest improvements. The advisors are expected to pass on these complaints and requests to the king. In this way, the king is aware of what the people want.

Today most monarchies have an elected **parliament** as well as a monarch. A parliament is a group of elected representatives. It is also the place where they meet, speak, and make decisions and laws for their country or province.

King Bhumibol Adulyadej of Thailand is the world's longest-ruling monarch. He appoints Thailand's prime minister from elected government representatives.

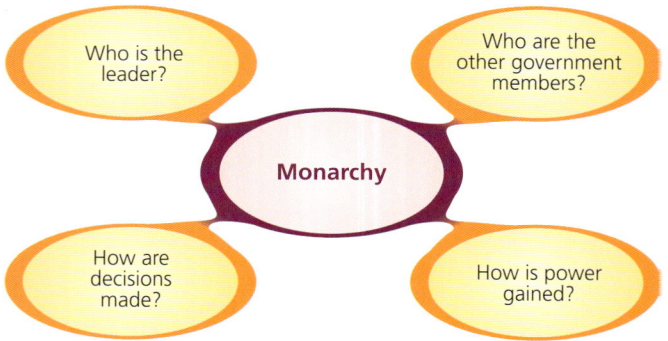

King Fahd bin Abd al-Aziz Al Saud of Saudi Arabia (right) meets with United States Secretary of Defense William S. Cohen (left) in 1998. The king appoints people to government, including many royal family members.

Dictatorship

In a **dictatorship**, the person leading the country makes all the laws and decisions. A dictator is not elected. Citizens are not asked their opinions on issues and are not allowed to criticize the government. Often dictators rely on the army to help them keep control over the country. These are called military dictators.

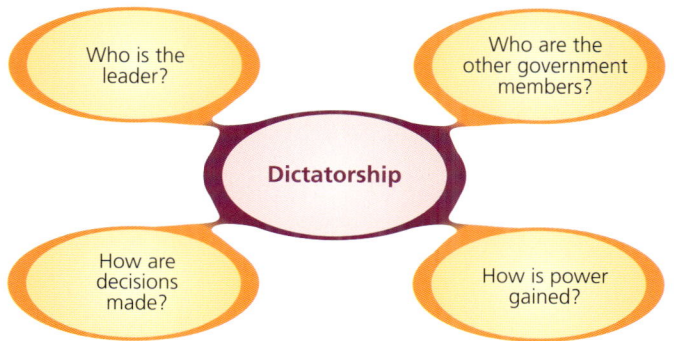

Fidel Castro has been the sole leader of Cuba since 1959.

Democracy

In a democracy, citizens of the country elect representatives who make laws and decisions based on the needs and wishes of the whole group. To make decisions that will benefit all of the citizens, the representatives consult with each other and with the citizens in the region they represent. Canada and New Zealand are examples of democracies.

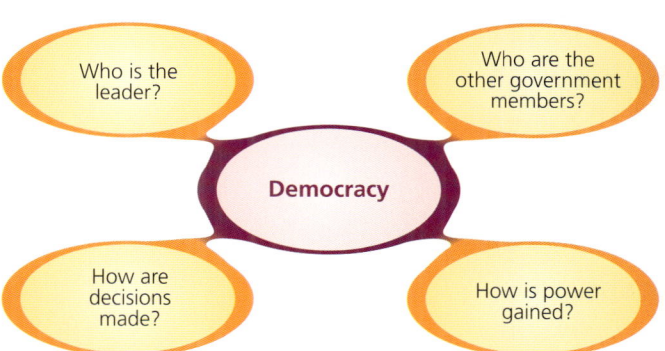

Helen Clark leads the democratic government of New Zealand. In this photo, she is visiting students in a school.

Do Discuss Discover

1. Copy this organizer about the types of government into your notebook. Leave room to write in each section. Complete your organizer using information on pages 12 and 13.

Type of Government	Monarchy	Dictatorship	Democracy
Who is the leader?			
Who are the other government members?			
How is power gained?			
How are decisions made?			
Examples (e.g., countries)			

Types of Democracy

Ancient Greece

About 2500 years ago, the government of Athens (a part of ancient Greece) was a type of limited democracy. Free men and women whose parents had been born in Athens were citizens of Athens. Male citizens could vote, help make laws, and own land. Female citizens could not take part in government.

Not everyone living in Athens at that time was considered a citizen. Slaves, people not born in Athens, and people who were captured in war could not be citizens.

In ancient Athens, male citizens were eligible to participate in government.

North American Aboriginal Nations

In historic times, an Aboriginal nation was made up of many small groups who had the same language and way of life and controlled a certain territory. Each village or camp of people normally had a leader or chief. The chief and some advisors made most of the decisions for their group. They listened to advice from all the other group members.

Decisions were usually made by **consensus**. Consensus means that everyone comes to an agreement on the choice or issue.

The Iroquois Confederacy, or the League of Five Nations, was a group of Aboriginal nations that formed a larger government. The Confederacy consisted of 50 chiefs who met once a year. They discussed issues that affected all of the nations in the Confederacy. Each nation was allowed one vote and all members had to agree with the decisions.

To make decisions by consensus, a group talks until everyone is able to agree.

Democracy in Canada

Canada is a modern democratic country. In Canada, all eligible citizens are expected to vote for government members. In turn, the people expect these elected representatives to make decisions based on what the voters want.

Citizens are free to discuss their ideas and the government's actions in public. If they are unhappy with the government, they work to change the government's decisions. For example, they make sure their opinions are known to the government through letters and public meetings. If they do not agree with how the government acts, they may try to elect someone different at the next election.

Paul Martin, Jr., a member of the Liberal Party, answers questions from citizens in Halifax.

Governing Bodies

Three groups in your class, each one acting as a different type of government, will build a structure following these steps:

1. The teacher will divide your class into three groups and appoint a governing body in each group. A governing body is a leader or leadership team.

   Group 1: The governing body is one person. He or she makes all the decisions without input from anyone else.

   Group 2: The governing body is three people. They make all the decisions without input from anyone else.

   Group 3: The governing body is all members of the group. They make the decisions together after much discussion.

2. The teacher will provide the governing body of each group with several clues that give hints about the structure that the group is supposed to build.

   In Groups 1 and 2, the governing body does not share the clues with anyone else. The governing body decides what the final structure will be and what materials the group needs. It gives the other members of the group directions for getting the materials and working together to create the structure.

   In Group 3, everyone is a part of the governing body. Everyone shares the clues and makes all decisions together.

3. Work with your group on your structure. Every few minutes, groups can exchange tools or materials. After 30 minutes, stop construction and view the structures as a class.

4. Individually, write a personal reflection on how your group worked together.

5. Discuss as a class how your groups worked together.

6. In your notebook, write a reflective paragraph explaining which of these types of government you think considers the needs of the group the most.

Sample Clues

I am strong enough to hold three textbooks.
I contain no glass parts.
I can be wide or narrow.
I must be made of at least ten different materials.
I must stand on something.
I don't lean on anything.
I can be tall or quite short.

Using Your Learning

Understanding Concepts

1. Put each vocabulary word (the words highlighted in red) from the Overview and this chapter on a file card. On each card, include the meaning, a picture or symbol, and a sentence containing the word. Organize the words alphabetically and use a file ring to hold them together. You will add words to your vocabulary file ring at the end of each chapter.

2. Complete a Venn diagram comparing democracy to either dictatorship or monarchy.

Developing Inquiry/Research and Communication Skills

3. Research a present-day government leader to find out how he/she came to power. Write a short biography. Include information about the type of government that he/she leads.

Developing Map/Globe Skills

4. Using an almanac for reference, find two examples of each of the three different types of government presented in this chapter. Plot the six locations on a map of the world. Remember to use a legend. Hint: Review the chart you did on page 13 to get you started.

Applying Concepts and Skills in Various Contexts

5. In small groups, role-play scenes to demonstrate how different governments would pass the following law: "The school year will be extended to 11 months."

6. Complete a personal reflection using this statement: "If I were leader of this country, the type of government I would run would be a … because …."

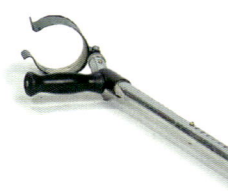

In Your Scrapbook

Your scrapbook project will be an on-going collection of items that show or tell about the government at work. You will summarize and reflect upon the chapter focus by collecting information from a variety of sources such as television newscasts, brochures, pictures, the Internet, or newspaper articles. You will also use the organizer model shown below. A sample of your work will be included for each chapter.

Chapter 1 Scrapbook Activity

1. Write Chapter 1 and its title at the top of the first page of your scrapbook.

2. Find a newspaper article written about the government in any country. Paste it in your scrapbook under the title.

3. Complete an organizer like the one below for your article. Add the organizer to your scrapbook.

Scrapbook Organizer

Chapter number and title	
Type of source (e.g., television newscast)	
Title or name (e.g., name of newspaper article)	
Location of the source (e.g., website address)	
Author or creator	
Date item was made or published	
Summary or description	
Personal reflection (related to the chapter focus)	

4. Add your reflective paragraph from the Governing Bodies activity on page 15 or another sample of your Chapter 1 work.

Reminder: Write the chapter number and title at the beginning of each chapter section in your scrapbook.

Chapter 2
Being a Citizen

Being a Canadian citizen means having certain rights and certain related responsibilities. These are written in Canada's laws, and they are also part of our customs and beliefs.

" Citizens of a country have the privileges and rights given to those who are part of their country. In return, they work to make their country better. Every year, people move to Canada from around the world. Most of them have heard about our way of life and the values that Canada represents. They apply to take our country's citizenship because they want to make Canada their home."

– *Andrew Newlin, Winnipeg, Manitoba*

" One of the many responsibilities of citizenship is to be informed about our government."

– *Maria Garcia, Victoria, British Columbia*

Focus on Learning

In this chapter, you will learn about
- Canadian citizenship
- the Canadian Charter of Rights and Freedoms
- rights and responsibilities
- volunteering

Vocabulary
- Confederation
- immigrant
- constitution
- amendment
- Canadian Charter of Rights and Freedoms

Citizens of Canada

In 1867, Ontario, Quebec, Nova Scotia, and New Brunswick joined together in **Confederation** to form the new country of Canada. After that, the four provinces of Canada had a central government and parliament, but Canada's laws and style of government were British. Canadians were still considered to be British subjects, not Canadian citizens.

Many **immigrants** came to Canada. Immigrants are people who choose to move to another country intending to stay and live there. More and more people moved to various parts of Canada, and more areas joined Confederation. By 1949, there were ten provinces and two territories in Canada.

Canada had become more active in the world. For example, thousands of Canadians fought in Europe during two world wars. Paul Martin, Sr., a member of the Canadian government, felt that the Canadian soldiers who died in World War II should be identified as Canadian citizens rather than British subjects.

In 1945, Paul Martin, Sr., and Prime Minister Mackenzie King presented the Canadian Citizenship Act to Parliament. It was passed on May 14, 1946, and took effect the next January. This meant that citizens were recognized as Canadian citizens and not British subjects.

As Canada continued to grow, changes to the Citizenship Act were needed. For example, in 1977, a new Citizenship Act lowered the number of years immigrants needed to wait before becoming citizens.

A Citizen stamp was issued in 1947 in honour of the Canadian Citizenship Act.

Citizenship Week

Citizenship Week is usually held in mid-October to celebrate the importance of citizenship. During this week in particular, Canadians reflect on the rights and responsibilities of being a citizen. They think about the need to build on positive things in Canadian communities.

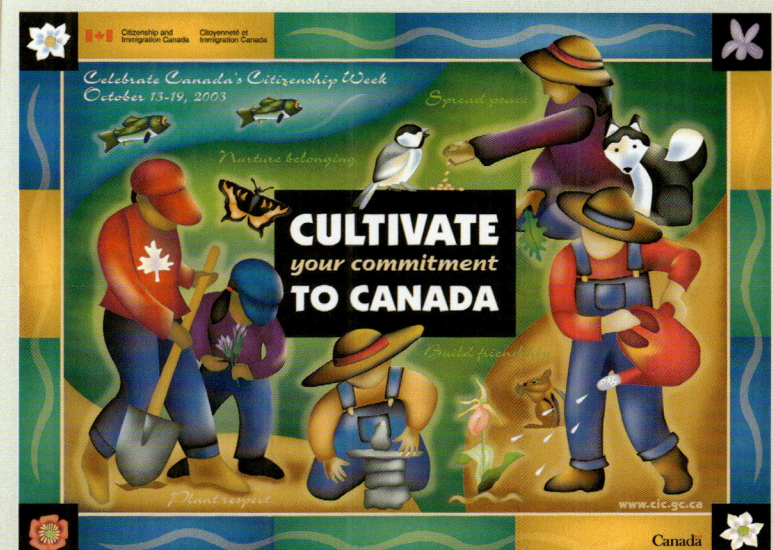

Do Discuss Discover

1. a) A new Citizen stamp could have many designs. Discuss possibilities with your classmates.
   b) What design would you choose for a new Citizen stamp?
2. In a small group, discuss ways you could celebrate Citizenship Week.

We Are Canadians

"The United Nations has formally recognized that Canada is one of the best countries in the world in which to live. Canada provides a high standard of living for its citizens. Most people who move here feel that Canada offers a better life for them and their children."

– *Morris Adams, St. John's, Newfoundland*

A View of Canada

Pope John Paul II attended World Youth Day hosted by Toronto in 2002. He described Canada as a caring country, rich with many cultures. He also noted that Canada has much to offer the world and is known for respecting and protecting people's rights.

"Canada is a peaceful, tolerant country that offers many freedoms and rights. Canada's laws need to support our goals and our values."

– *Ellen Barnes, Yellowknife, Northwest Territories*

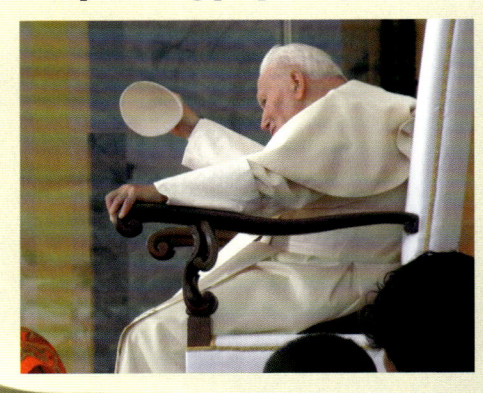

"Our flag, our national anthem, the maple leaf, the coat of arms, the Parliament buildings, and the bright uniforms of RCMP officers are all symbols of Canada. I feel proud and happy when people from other countries recognize them."

– *Alex Tran, Kitchener, Ontario*

"I think our national symbols encourage us to be active, participating citizens of our country. I believe that, as Canadian citizens, we need to show through our actions the things that we think are important. For example, we can volunteer time to help in our communities."

– *Émilie Turcotte, Quebec City, Quebec*

Do Discuss Discover

1. a) Work with a partner to brainstorm goals and values you both think Canadians have.
   b) Individually, decide on one you think is very important. Create a bumper sticker about your idea.
2. Review Getting Information from Quotations on page 11.
   a) Is the information about Pope John Paul II's statements a direct quotation or reported speech?
   b) Select one direct quotation from this page. Re-write it to make it into reported speech.

The Canadian Charter of Rights and Freedoms

In 1867, the British government passed a law called the British North America (BNA) Act that changed the way Canada was governed. The BNA Act was Canada's first **constitution**. A constitution is a written set of rules explaining how a country will be governed.

In 1982, some **amendments**, or changes, were made to the BNA Act. One of them gave Canada the right to change the constitution without asking permission from the British parliament. The other change was to add the **Canadian Charter of Rights and Freedoms** to Canada's constitution. It is a document that lists the rights of Canadian citizens in order to protect them by law.

Citizens have both rights and responsibilities. For example, eligible Canadian citizens have the right to vote in elections. They also have the responsibility to become informed about the issues and the people seeking election, and to vote for the person they think will do the best job. You will learn more about voting and elections in the coming chapters.

Queen Elizabeth II, next to Prime Minister Trudeau, signs the Constitution Act of 1982, officially proclaiming changes to the BNA Act.

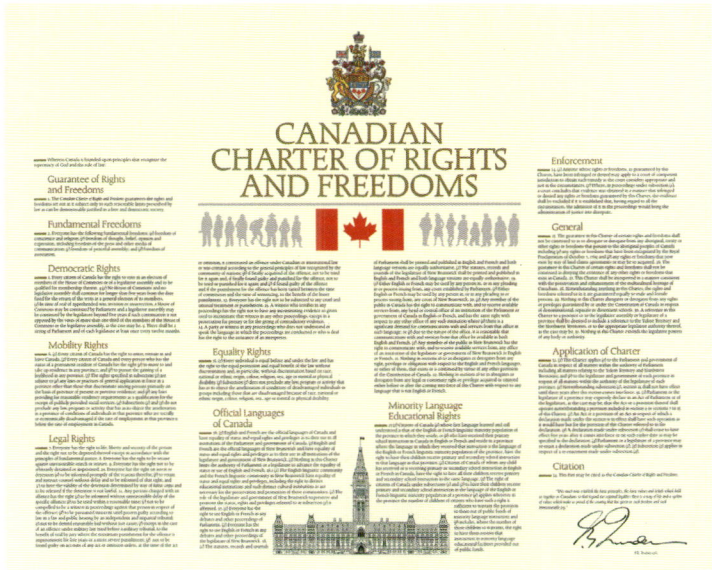

The Charter forms the basis of Canada's democracy by protecting the rights and freedoms of all Canadians.

" The Charter [of Rights and Freedoms] is a uniquely Canadian document and a product of our distinctive history. It is also the product, not just of politicians, but of ordinary Canadians who worked tirelessly to ensure that it would reflect their vision of Canada—a Canada that recognizes respectful tolerance of one another, the interests of individuals as well as groups, and the balance between individual rights and the well-being of the country as a whole. "

– *The Right Honourable Chief Justice of Canada Beverley McLachlin*

A Canadian Citizen's Rights

The Canadian Charter of Rights and Freedoms presents a Canadian citizen's rights in a number of different categories: fundamental freedom rights, democratic rights, mobility rights, legal rights, equality rights, language rights, and the enforcement of these rights.

- **Fundamental Freedom Rights**
  - to practise your religion
  - to have and express your opinion
  - to meet in peaceful groups
  - to belong to any group

- **Democratic Rights**
  - to vote in elections
  - to participate in regular elections
  - to run for election

- **Mobility Rights**
  - to enter or leave Canada as you wish
  - to move and live in any province within Canada

- **Legal Rights**
  - to feel free and safe
  - to have a fair trial within a reasonable time
  - to have an interpreter if the language is not understood

- **Equality Rights**
  - to live free of discrimination and prejudice

- **Language Rights**
  - to communicate with services provided by the Canadian government in either official language (French or English)
  - to have children in school taught in either language

I'm a Canadian

I have the right to speak my mind

I'm a Canadian

I have the right to stand out

I'm a Canadian

I have the right to be free

I'm a Canadian

I have the power inside to do my country good

I'm a Canadian

I have the honour to say

I'm a Canadian

– *by Ashlee Clarke*

- **Enforcement Rights**
  - to go to court if any of these rights are denied

Do Discuss Discover

1. a) In a small group, discuss the rights included in one of the categories. Come up with examples.
   b) In your notebook, create a billboard design for one of the rights in the category.

Children Have Rights, Too!

Although many children around the world are treated well, some are not. Some of their basic needs are not being met. Because of this, the United Nations created a document called the United Nations Rights of the Child.

The United Nations Rights of the Child clearly lists the rights that all children around the world should have. The following are some of the rights listed.

Children have the right to

- proper food and medicine
- schools
- special care if needed
- love and understanding.

The United Nations Universal Declaration of Human Rights was proclaimed in 1948. It begins by saying,

"All human beings are born free and equal in dignity and rights."

Do Discuss Discover

1. Look at the pictures on this page. In your notebook, list the rights that are being shown in each picture.

Responsibilities of Citizenship

People who choose to live in Canada are expected to take the responsibilities of citizenship seriously in order to live freely and in harmony with others. Responsible and active citizens can help make this country an even better place to live.

Responsibilities of Citizens

- obey the laws of the country
- show respect for all individuals
- respect the private property of others
- understand that public property exists for the benefit of all members of society
- learn about Canada's history and political system
- learn one of Canada's two official languages
- be an informed voter and vote in elections

Around the World

One responsibility of citizens of Israel is to serve in the army. They are trained to do so when they are 18. Eligible women then serve in the army for 21 months and men serve for three years. Until age 55, men can be called back to duty for up to 45 days a year. Unmarried women can be called back as well, but rarely are.

Do Discuss Discover

1. Review the rights and responsibilities of citizens listed on pages 22 to 25. In a small group, discuss which rights and responsibilities are being shown in the images below. Individually, sketch two different sets of rights and responsibilities in your notebook.

Rights   **Responsibilities**

Volunteers

Canadians of all ages help create a sense of community by volunteering their time and helping those around them.

Volunteers at the humane society help exercise and care for animals.

Library volunteers help children enjoy and read books.

Volunteers share their knowledge about various topics such as wildlife and their habitats.

Legacy

I am going your way.
Let me help you along.
You seem to be tired
And my arms are strong.

Let me carry your load.
I'm up to the test.
I'll shoulder your burden
And give you a rest.

I was once troubled
With problems and grief
'Til a friend helped me closely
And offered relief.

And all that friend asked
Before he was gone
Was when I felt better
I pass his help on.

– by Anne Brandt

Samantha Moonsammy, Volunteer

On April 21, 1999, Samantha Moonsammy's name was called and she walked to the front of the room. All eyes were on her as she was presented with the Ontario Medal for Young Volunteers in recognition of her work in her community.

Samantha volunteered with many different organizations that served senior citizens, youth, and people in need. Members of the community nominated her for the award because they wanted her to know how much her contributions were appreciated.

Do Discuss Discover

1. Discuss the message of the poem on this page. What kind of help is being offered? Why was this help being offered?
2. Create an acrostic-style poem using either the word Citizenship or Volunteer.

Designing a T-Shirt for Volunteers

You will need
- pencil
- wax crayons
- white paper
- white T-shirt (cotton/polyester blend works best)
- iron and ironing board
- wax paper
- cloth or dishtowel

1. Decide on the purpose of the message on your T-shirt about volunteering. For example, will you encourage people to volunteer or will you celebrate the contributions made by volunteers?
2. Create your picture, design, or symbol with a pencil and crayons on a sheet of paper. Give extra attention to the lettering. For example, will you outline or colour the letters to make them stand out?
3. Once you are satisfied with the paper design, draw and colour your design on the T-shirt using wax crayons.
4. Place your T-shirt on a table or ironing board. Insert a piece of clean white paper inside the T-shirt under the coloured area.
5. Place wax paper on top of the crayon design on the T-shirt, and then place a cloth or dishtowel on top of that.
6. With your teacher's help, heat the iron to low or medium heat. Run the iron over the cloth several times to melt the crayon marks into place.

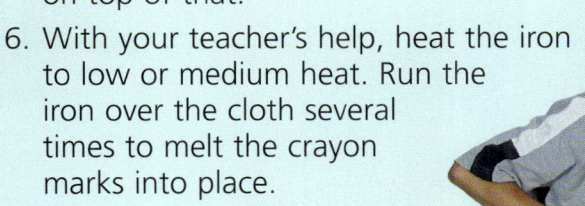

Using Your Learning

Understanding Concepts

1. Make file cards for each of the Chapter 2 vocabulary words. (See question 1 on page 16.)

2. Create a rights and responsibilities organizer like this one using the rights identified on pages 22 and 23.

Right	Responsibility
the right to vote	to make an informed choice at every election

Developing Inquiry/Research and Communication Skills

3. a) Go to www.ainc-inac.gc.ca/ks/pdf/e_guide3.pdf to find "The Learning Circle." Locate information about the Declaration of the First Nations on page 56 of the document.

   b) Create a rights and responsibilities organizer in your notebook similar to the one in question 2.

Applying Concepts and Skills in Various Contexts

4. Create a commercial that encourages people to become more active citizens in their communities. Remember that your message needs to be seen and heard. You may want to add music or sound effects to your presentation.

5. Visit www.unicef.ca/eng/unicef/sch_election/giraffe1.html to find a version of the United Nations Convention on the Rights of the Child.

   a) In a small group, discuss which rights are most important to you.

   b) List the rights your group feels would be important to you in school.

   c) With your classmates, discuss the rights you listed and then create a Charter of Rights for your class.

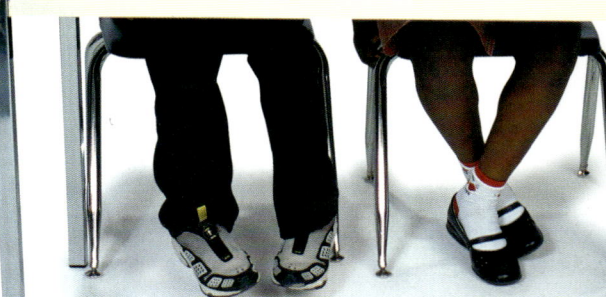

In Your Scrapbook

1. Choose one of these:

    a) Visit www.volunteer.ca. Find "Celebrating volunteers" and click on "Share your volunteering stories." Write a short summary about one volunteer's story.

    b) Find a newspaper article about being an active or responsible citizen.

2. Add your summary or the article to your scrapbook.

3. Complete an organizer. (See page 17.) Add it to your scrapbook.

4. Add a sample of Chapter 2 work such as your Charter of Rights from question 5 on page 28.

World Expo Link

Whenever a country is given the opportunity to host an event like a World Exposition, citizens of that country become involved. The preparation must begin many years before the actual event. One thing that must be decided upon is the theme of the exposition. In this activity, you will develop a theme for your city's exposition.

1. As a class, discuss and list the kinds of things that are important to Canadians. Think about things that you, your friends, and adults around you value and appreciate about Canada.

2. In your small project group, look through newspapers for headlines that reflect the values of Canadian citizens today. Cut out the headlines and discuss them.

3. With your project group, write themes that could be used for your World Exposition.

4. Discuss and select one theme for your World Exposition proposal.

Chapter 3
Becoming a Citizen

Canada receives immigrants from around the world. They leave their countries and come to Canada for many reasons. Immigrants bring with them a variety of customs, lifestyles, and expectations. They learn about Canadian life and share their way of life with other Canadians. When they have met the requirements, they can attend a citizenship court and become Canadian citizens.

" My family and I came to Canada four years ago from New Delhi. My father is an engineer and my mother takes care of my sisters and me. We go to school and attend after-school classes in swimming, sports, and music. We have found many friends here in Sarnia.

" My family has received our "Notice to Appear to Take the Oath of Citizenship." Becoming a citizen takes some time and some studying to learn about this country. We have followed all of the necessary steps and now we are going to become Canadian citizens! "

– *Shellina Gupta, Sarnia, Ontario*

Focus on Learning

In this chapter, you will learn about
- immigrating to Canada
- becoming a Canadian citizen
- reading statistics and drawing conclusions

Vocabulary
- landed immigrant
- refugee
- affirmation
- naturalized citizen
- multicultural

" I think I'm privileged to meet these people who come from all over the world. Everybody is just delighted and happy to be a citizen of Canada. "

– *Ruth Cruden, Citizenship Judge*

" There are times I am speechless, when I can barely say 'Congratulations' to these happy people. It is so wonderful to grant them such a gift. "

– *Roberto Roberti, Citizenship Judge*

Immigrating to Canada

People leave their countries for many reasons. Some leave because they feel that they can have a better way of life somewhere else. Others want to be with relatives who have already moved to another country. Still others leave a country that is experiencing war or other tensions. Some leave because it is too dangerous to stay.

Once people from other countries are officially accepted as immigrants, they are called **landed immigrants**. That means they legally live in Canada and can prepare to apply for Canadian citizenship. **Refugees** apply to be landed immigrants after they have arrived in Canada. Refugees are people who go to another country for safety and security.

Number of Immigrants by Top Ten Source Countries

COUNTRY	2001 Number
China	40 296
India	27 812
Pakistan	15 339
Philippines	12 903
Korea	9 604
United States	5 894
Iran	5 736
Romania	5 585
Sri Lanka	5 514
United Kingdom	5 345

Citizenship and Immigration Canada

"My grandfather left his homeland because he wanted to live in a country where he would be able to find work and raise a family."

– *Elena Mammone, Calgary, Alberta*

"We moved to Canada because my aunts and uncles were here and we wanted to be with the rest of our family."

– *Arjun Bharuta, Sudbury, Ontario*

"My family and others with the same religious beliefs had to meet secretly in one another's homes to pray and talk. We were not allowed to practise our religion freely. Coming to Canada means we are able to openly practise our religion."

– *Herman Solse, Vancouver, British Columbia*

"For many years my country had been at war. My family came to Canada because they wanted to live peacefully."

– *Sarah Naardan, Whitehorse, Yukon Territory*

Do Discuss Discover

1. a) Locate key words or phrases about the reasons people leave their birth countries.
   b) Make a web of reasons why people immigrate to Canada.

Preparing to Immigrate

Before they leave their country of origin, people

- usually apply to be landed immigrants of Canada. People who have children complete applications for those who are under 18.
- prepare to submit any documents that are needed
- try to learn one of the languages of Canada—English or French
- should be aware that they will be given a medical examination to check on their health
- should be aware that their health and personal background will be checked (e.g., for a criminal record)
- must have enough money to pay the processing fees and to live on until they are settled.

Completing these requirements in advance makes immigrating to Canada easier.

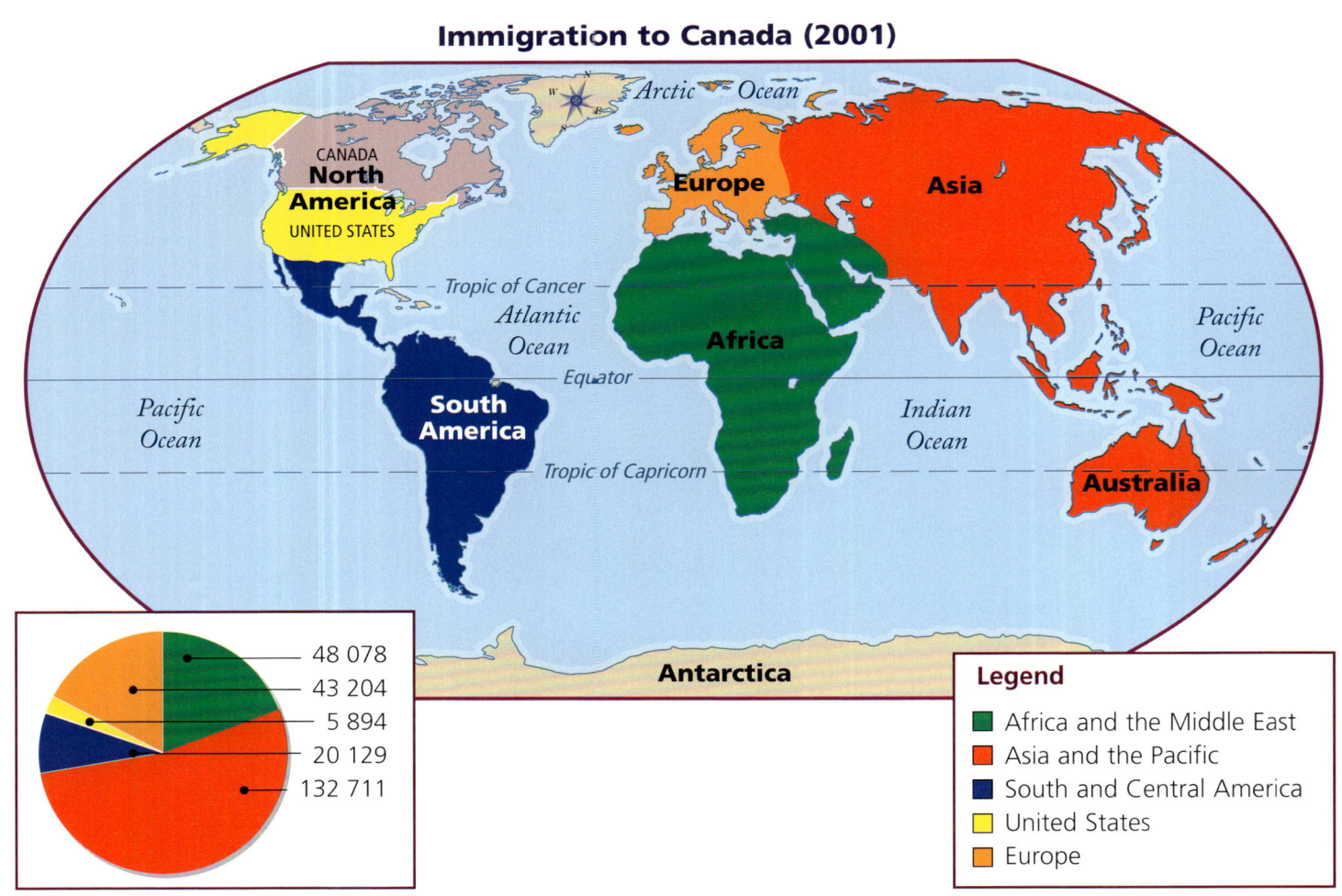

Immigration to Canada (2001)

- 48 078
- 43 204
- 5 894
- 20 129
- 132 711

Legend
- Africa and the Middle East
- Asia and the Pacific
- South and Central America
- United States
- Europe

Report from a Host Family

Our family really enjoys being part of the volunteer host program. We help people who have recently immigrated to get settled in our community.

Families who are new to Canada sometimes have a hard time getting used to their new home and our culture. They experience many different feelings about the changes in their lives.

My family has a great time showing them around the neighbourhood. Sometimes we take them for walking tours to show them where stores and services can be found. If they have trouble understanding forms or letters to which they must respond, we help them.

The best part is that each family we meet develops into a new friendship. They appreciate the ways we help them, and we learn a lot about them and the part of the world they came from. Sometimes we have dinner together. We introduce them to our foods, like roast beef and potatoes, and they introduce us to foods that they make.

We like hearing about and seeing pictures of their birth countries. We might not ever get to travel to that country, but we feel like we know it a little. The host program is a wonderful experience for all those involved.

Many Canadian provinces have host programs or settlement services to help newcomers feel welcome.

Host program volunteers either answer questions for new arrivals or put them in touch with someone who can help them.

Volunteers are sometimes assigned to newcomers with the same interests. They spend a few hours each week with them.

Do Discuss Discover

1. In a group of four or five students, discuss ways in which people can be made to feel welcome. You may discuss how certain actions, words in English or different languages, and activities make people feel like they belong and are appreciated.

Becoming a Canadian Citizen

A person wishing to become a Canadian citizen must plan and prepare. Once the basic requirements are met, she or he is ready to take the final steps toward citizenship by completing the application process.

Applying for Citizenship

There are a number of steps for completing a citizenship application.

To Prepare for Canadian Citizenship:
- live in Canada as a landed immigrant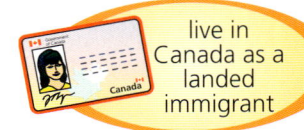
- live three years as a permanent resident
- speak English or French
- gain knowledge of Canada's history, geography, and government
- attend citizenship class or study citizenship booklet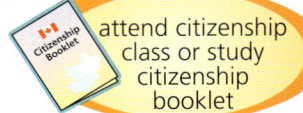

1. Complete the "Application for Citizenship" form. (Make sure separate forms are completed for each child.)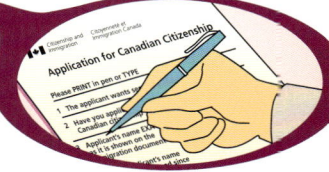

2. Include the proper documents:
   - a photocopy of the immigration landing record
   - photocopies of two pieces of identification.

3. Include two colour or black-and-white photographs stamped by the photographer and signed by the applicant.

4. Include the non-refundable application processing fee and the Right of Citizenship fee.

5. Mail the application form, documents, and fees to Citizenship and Immigration Canada.

6. Complete and pass the written or oral test.

7. If successful, the applicant takes the Oath of Citizenship and receives her/his certificate.

Making a Citizenship Banner

Work by yourself to create a banner to welcome new citizens of Canada.

You will need

- sheet of paper (about 22 cm x 36 cm)
- piece of felt fabric (about 22 cm x 36 cm)
- crayons
- ruler and chalk
- scissors and glue
- smaller pieces of felt fabric in various colours
- string or stick

1. Decide on the shape of your banner. It could be square, rectangular, or triangular. Think about symbols, words, or scenes that would welcome new citizens.
2. Draw and colour your banner design on the piece of paper. Save this copy for your scrapbook.
3. Choose a piece of felt fabric for your banner. Use a ruler and some chalk to outline the shape of your banner on the felt.
4. Cut out your banner.
5. As a class, share leftover pieces of felt to decorate your banners. Choose small pieces of felt in other colours to cut out letters, pictures, and symbols.
6. After cutting out all the pieces you need, arrange them on your banner. Lift one piece at a time, dot glue on the back, and lay the piece on the banner. Carefully pat it and let it dry.
7. Attach loops of felt or fold the edge of your banner over a string or stick to display it.

Reading Statistics and Drawing Conclusions

Statistics are collections of factual information in numbers. Charts are an organized way of showing how different statistics compare with each other.

One type of statistical chart compares numbers of people at different times, as shown in the example below. This chart displays how numbers changed over time showing the **patterns** of immigration.

Example:

When you read and interpret the chart below, here are some steps to follow:

1. Read the title—it tells what statistics are being displayed.

2. Find out the source of the statistics. Is this a **reliable source**? Can you count on the numbers being as correct as possible? For example, Statistics Canada is a reliable source.

3. Note how the statistics are organized. For example, on the chart to the right, the "People who immigrate" is displayed by "Year."

4. Look at how the information is displayed. For example, dates should be displayed in sequence from the earliest to the most recent date. They should be spaced at regular intervals.

Immigrants to Canada in Ten Years (1984–1993)

YEAR	People who immigrate*
1984	88 000
1985	84 000
1986	99 000
1987	152 000
1988	162 000
1989	192 000
1990	214 000
1991	231 000
1992	253 000
1993	256 000

*rounded to nearest thousand
Table G2, Citizenship and Immigration Statistics 1996

5. Study the statistics.
   - What patterns do they show? Do the numbers increase regularly, decrease regularly, or are they irregular?
   - Is there a **trend**—a steady change?
   - Are there **exceptions**—numbers that don't fit a trend?

6. Look at the exceptions. Do you have any information about why this happened? Maybe you will need to do more research to find a reason.

7. Make predictions about what is likely to happen in later years. Base your prediction on the pattern shown in the chart.

Some Trends in Citizenship

Landed immigrants can apply to become Canadian citizens after they live in Canada for three years. Not all landed immigrants apply for citizenship right away. Sometimes they live in Canada for many years without applying.

Landed immigrants have the right to work and the right to own property. They have the right to healthcare benefits, education for their children, and most other benefits of citizenship. If they carry proof of their status with them, landed immigrants can return to Canada after they travel outside of the country.

A small number of landed immigrants change their minds about living in Canada. They may return to their birth country or move somewhere else.

Around the World

To become a citizen of Chile, adult applicants must have a permanent residence permit. They must live in Chile for at least five uninterrupted years and must be able to earn a living. Also, they need the permission of the Minister of the Interior. Convicted criminals are not eligible to become citizens.

> "Canada has a unique model of citizenship, based on diversity and mutual responsibility. This model requires deliberate efforts to connect Canadians across their differences, to link them to their history, and to enable their diverse voices to participate in choosing the Canada we want."
>
> – Adrienne Clarkson, Governor General, Throne Speech, September 30, 2002

Do Discuss Discover

1. Review page 36. Follow the steps for reading statistics and drawing conclusions.

Persons Granted Canadian Citizenship in Ten Years* (1987–1996)

YEAR	People who became citizens*
1987	74 000
1988	59 000
1989	87 000
1990	104 000
1991	119 000
1992	116 000
1993	151 000
1994	217 000
1995	228 000
1996	156 000

Table 1, Citizenship and Immigration Statistics 1996

*rounded to nearest thousand

2. Answer these questions in your notebook.
    a) Compare this chart with the chart on page 36. What trends do you see in each? What exceptions do you see in each chart? How are the trends similar in the two charts? How are they different?
    b) Compare the number of immigrants in each year with the number of citizenships granted three years afterwards. With a partner, discuss the patterns.
    c) Write a concluding statement for the chart above.

Each year, thousands of people officially accept the rights and responsibilities of citizenship when they become Canadian citizens.

Citizenship Affirmation Ceremony

After successfully completing either written or oral questioning, citizenship candidates are invited to attend a ceremony to take the Oath of Citizenship. This is also called the swearing-in or **affirmation** ceremony. When making this affirmation, a person is stating their agreement to the rights and responsibilities of citizenship. It is the last step in becoming a **naturalized citizen**. A naturalized citizen is an immigrant who has received Canadian citizenship.

There are many VIPs (Very Important Persons) involved in the affirmation ceremony. Each of the people attending has a specific responsibility.

Performers are often invited to add to the celebration. They show Canada's multicultural society.

Clerk of the Court guides the procedure of the ceremony. She/He makes sure that all the legal requirements of the Citizenship Act are properly met.

Presiding Officer delivers the opening speech, administers the Oath of Citizenship, which is spoken in both official languages, congratulates the new citizens, and presents the citizenship certificates. The presiding officer is usually a Citizenship Court Judge. He or she may be available for photographs afterwards.

Candidates take the Oath of Citizenship and receive their Certificates of Citizenship and a copy of the Canadian Charter of Rights and Freedoms. Many candidates bring members of their families or friends to witness this special occasion.

Members of the media may be present. All new citizens are informed and are asked to sign a media release form before the ceremony. That way pictures of the ceremony and the citizens can be shown in newspapers or on the news.

Special guests may attend, such as members of the three levels of government or community leaders. They may speak for a short time to offer congratulations to all the new citizens.

Master of Ceremonies begins the ceremony and introduces any special guests that are present. He or she may be a representative of a community group.

" I swear (or affirm) that I will be faithful and bear true allegiance to Her Majesty Queen Elizabeth the Second, Queen of Canada, Her Heirs and Successors, and that I will faithfully observe the laws of Canada and fulfil my duties as a Canadian citizen. "

– *Oath of Citizenship*

Royal Canadian Mounted Police Officer opens the ceremony by leading the Presiding Officer, Clerk of the Court, and special guests into the room. He or she wears the formal red serge uniform and represents Canadian law enforcement.

Host groups provide a space for the ceremony and sponsor, help organize, and prepare for the ceremony and the reception. Host groups may include schools, service clubs, volunteer groups, non-profit organizations, or levels of government.

Do Discuss Discover

1. Create an organizer, or use one given to you by your teacher, to summarize each of the descriptions of people and events. Match them with the numbered photographs. Some photographs and descriptions may have more than one match, and some descriptions may not match a photograph.

Reaffirmation Ceremony

The reaffirmation ceremony allows those who are already citizens of Canada to accept again the rights and responsibilities of being Canadian citizens. This ceremony is much like the affirmation ceremony, but it does not require a Citizenship Court Judge or RCMP officer to be present. A Citizenship and Immigration official may be invited. The ceremony can be held at a community location such as your school.

This ceremony includes

- a welcome
- opening remarks from the Presiding Officer or leaders
- speeches or presentations
- administering the Oath of Canadian Citizenship in both languages
- singing "O Canada"
- a closing.

O Canada!

O Canada!
Our home and native
  land!
True patriot love
  in all thy sons
  command.
With glowing hearts
  we see thee rise,
The True North strong
  and free!
From far and wide
  O Canada,
we stand on guard
  for thee.
God keep our land
  glorious and free!
O Canada, we stand on
  guard for thee.
O Canada, we stand on
  guard for thee.

O Canada!

O Canada!
Terre de nos aïeux,
Ton front est ceint
  de fleurons glorieux!
Car ton bras sait porter
  l'épée,
Il sait porter la croix!
Ton histoire est une
  épopée
Des plus brillants
  exploits.
Et ta valeur, de foi
  trempée,
Protégera nos foyers et
  nos droits.
Protégera nos foyers et
  nos droits.

Do Discuss Discover

1. Think about the reasons your class might have for participating in a reaffirmation ceremony. In your notebook, write five words to describe how you might feel about taking part in this ceremony.

We Celebrate Our Citizens!

On July 1, 2001, the new *Spirit of Canada* coin was unveiled. It is the third coloured coin issued by the Royal Canadian Mint. The coin was designed by Silke Ware, an artist from Kitchener, Ontario. It presents themes that are important to Canadian citizens: children, hope for the future, and a supportive society.

Canadian Mosaic

Canada is a **multicultural** country. People of many cultural backgrounds maintain and freely share their culture, customs, ideas, and beliefs. The right to freely hold and share one's ideas and beliefs is important to people around the world. This is demonstrated by the great numbers of immigrants who arrive in Canada each year.

"Canada's history is one of welcoming people from around the world to share in our Canadian mosaic."

– *Emmanuel Triassi, Chairperson of the Board of Directors for the Royal Canadian Mint*

In Canada's multicultural society, people are encouraged to maintain their culture and customs. One example is Toronto's Chinatown.

"Canada asks no citizens to deny their forebears, to forsake their inheritance—only that each should accept and value the cultural freedom of others as he enjoys his own. It is a gentle invitation, this call to citizenship and I urge those who have accepted the invitation to participate fully in the building of the Canadian society."

– *Queen Elizabeth II, 1973*

Canadians enjoy a wide variety of cultural experiences from around the world. Every summer, Toronto hosts the Caribana Festival, a celebration of Caribbean culture.

Do Discuss Discover

1. As a class, discuss the cultural groups represented in your classroom community.
2. Write an explanation, in your own words, of what Queen Elizabeth II meant when she said "participate fully in the building of the Canadian society."

Using Your Learning

Understanding Concepts

1. Make file cards for each of the Chapter 3 vocabulary words. (See question 1 on page 16.)
2. In your notebook, outline the steps for applying for citizenship.
3. Using a Venn Diagram, compare the affirmation (swearing-in) ceremony and the reaffirmation ceremony.

Developing Inquiry/Research and Communication Skills

4. Visit www.citzine.ca/stuff.php?lng-e and choose "Cool Canadians." Write a paragraph telling how one "Cool Canadian" citizen contributed to the community.

Developing Map/Globe Skills

5. a) On a world map, colour the countries from which each of your classmates and their families originally came. Create a legend for your map.

   b) Write two statements about immigration to Canada.

Applying Concepts and Skills in Various Contexts

6. Discuss ways that your community reflects the multicultural image of Canada. Cut advertisements from newspapers, grocery flyers, and magazines that reflect this. Glue them in your notebook.
7. Create a word collage of what being a Canadian citizen means to you. Use a variety of colours, designs, and letter sizes.
8. a) Think about how new citizens feel, what it means to be a citizen of Canada, and the contributions they make.

   b) Write and present a short speech of congratulations that could be given at a citizenship affirmation ceremony.
9. On a piece of art paper, create and colour a symbol that welcomes people to your class. Cut it out and hang it outside the classroom door.

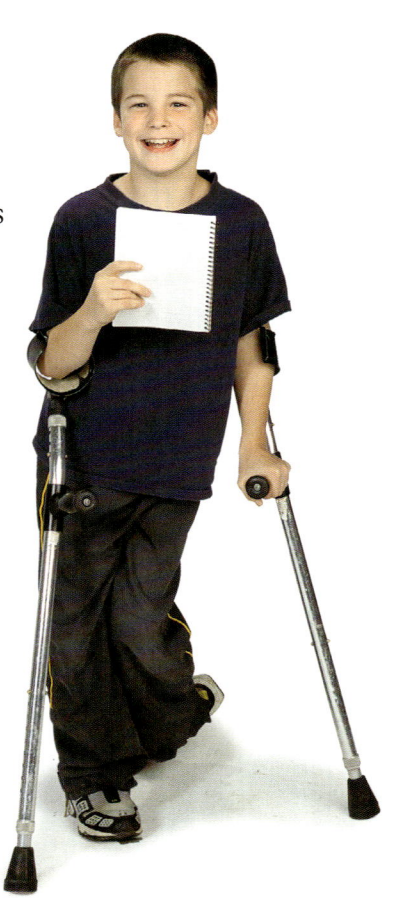

In Your Scrapbook

1. Choose one of these options:

   a) Look in a Canadian almanac. Make a statistical chart showing how many people immigrated to Ontario in the last five years.

   b) Find a magazine or newspaper article about citizenship or use the items you collected for question 6 on page 42.

2. Add your chart, article, or advertisements to your scrapbook.

3. Complete an organizer. (See page 17.) Add it to your scrapbook.

4. Include the paper copy of your citizenship banner or another sample of your Chapter 3 work.

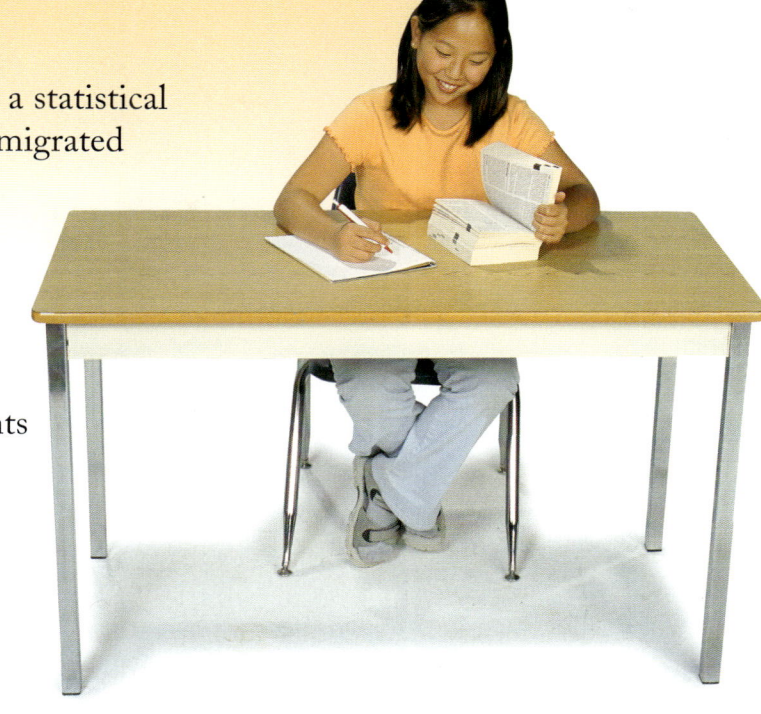

World Expo Link

Recall the reasons why many immigrants are attracted to Canada. A city preparing a proposal for an international event must show that their city offers many attractions and will be the best host for the event and international guests.

1. As a class, discuss how a city could draw tourists to its World Exposition.

2. In your project group, use travel and library books, as well as the Internet, to research your selected city. List attractions that visitors to your city could enjoy.

3. Create a poster with your group. Show that your city is the best place for the World Exposition by highlighting its best attractions.

Chapter 4
Levels of Government

There are three levels of elected Canadian governments: municipal, provincial/territorial, and federal. This chapter will review the first two of these levels. The remaining chapters of this textbook will focus on the federal government.

"From the outset, our government made a commitment to put the residents of Nunavut and the natural environment at the centre of our work in developing the territory."

– *Paul Okalik, first Premier of Nunavut, elected March 5, 1999*

"Our city is a first class city with a strong history of good governance and commitment to our citizens… I am very proud of the way our city has grown and matured…"

– *Hazel McCallion, longest-serving mayor of Mississauga, first elected in 1978*

Focus on Learning

In this chapter, you will learn about
- Canada's system of three levels of government
- municipal government
- asking questions to gather information
- provincial and territorial governments
- Aboriginal self-government

Vocabulary
- federal government
- municipal government
- reeve
- mayor
- councillor
- ward
- bylaw
- Lieutenant-Governor
- Premier
- Cabinet
- Legislative Assembly
- judiciary
- riding
- candidate
- political party
- bill
- self-government

Separate and Shared

The governing of Canada is split among three levels of government: the central **federal government**, the regional governments of the provinces and territories, and a large number of local **municipal governments**.

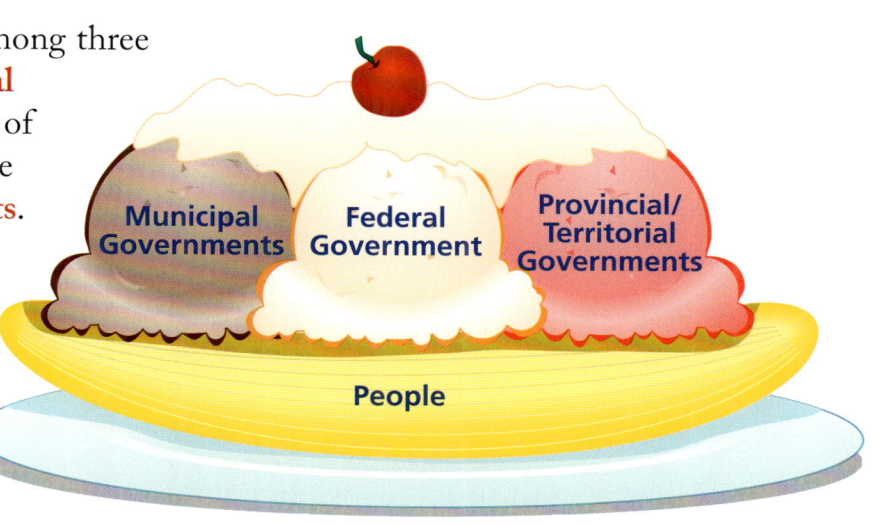

The federal government makes and enforces laws for the whole country. It sets up and runs national government programs for all Canadians. Some examples are the Canada Child Tax Benefit, Canada Pension Plan, Old Age Security, and Citizenship and Immigration Canada.

The governments of the thirteen provinces and territories make laws and run programs for the people living in them. For example, provincial and territorial governments are responsible for schools and healthcare programs.

There are thousands of municipal governments in Canada. Cities, towns, villages, counties, and districts have municipal governments that represent and serve the needs of local citizens. For example, they are responsible for snow removal, parking, and pet laws.

Some of the responsibilities of the three levels of government in Canada are separate, and some are shared. For example, the armed forces are a responsibility of the federal government alone. However, all three levels of government share the costs of building and looking after roads.

Some laws apply to the whole country and some only to a region or a local area. For example, Canada's criminal laws apply to the whole country, but laws about the hours that stores are open are local.

Do Discuss Discover

1. Re-read the quotations on page 44. What does Hazel McCallion value? What is important to Nunavut's government?
2. Canada's system of government has three levels. A school system has at least three parts as well: the school board, schools, and classrooms.
   a) Think about the responsibilities of each level of government. Think about the roles of each part of a school system. Match each level of government with one part of the school system.
   b) Give a reason for each match.

Municipal Governments
Federal Government
Provincial/ Territorial Governments
People

Municipal Government

A municipal government serves some of the group needs of the people who live in a place or area that is defined by a boundary. Municipalities can be either urban or rural. They may have a large population in a small space or a small population in a large space. Cities, towns, villages, counties, and municipal districts are all municipalities. Ontario has 447 municipalities.

A council, whether rural or urban, governs each municipality. The head of the local council of a rural municipality or town is often called a **reeve**. The head of a city council is a **mayor**. Members of a council are called **councillors**.

The flow chart on this page shows an example of the structure of a municipal government of a city.

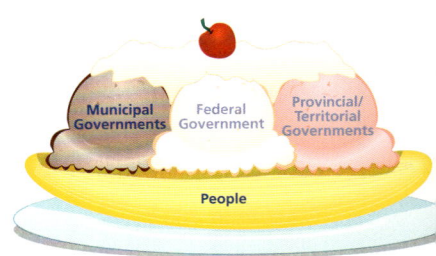

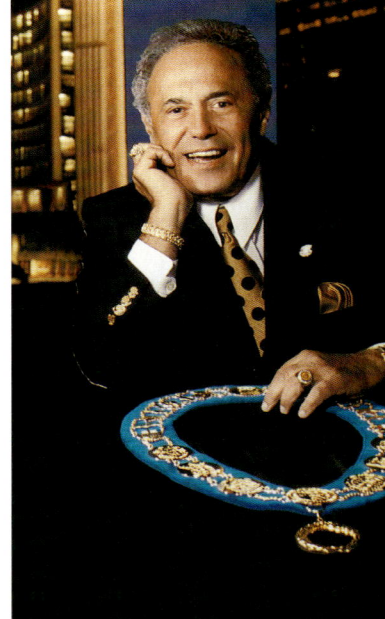

Mel Lastman first became mayor of Toronto in 1998 after having served as mayor of North York for 25 years.

Structure of a Municipal Government

Mayor
Council
Town Clerk
Planning Committee
Operations Committee
Chief Administrator
Fire Department
fights fires, does fire inspections
Economic Development
assists businesses and attracts new businesses
Parks & Recreation
builds, maintains, and runs recreational facilities
Planning
plans work done by the municipality
Public Works
builds and maintains public buildings, roads, etc.
Treasury
takes in money through taxes and fees; pays out public money to provide services

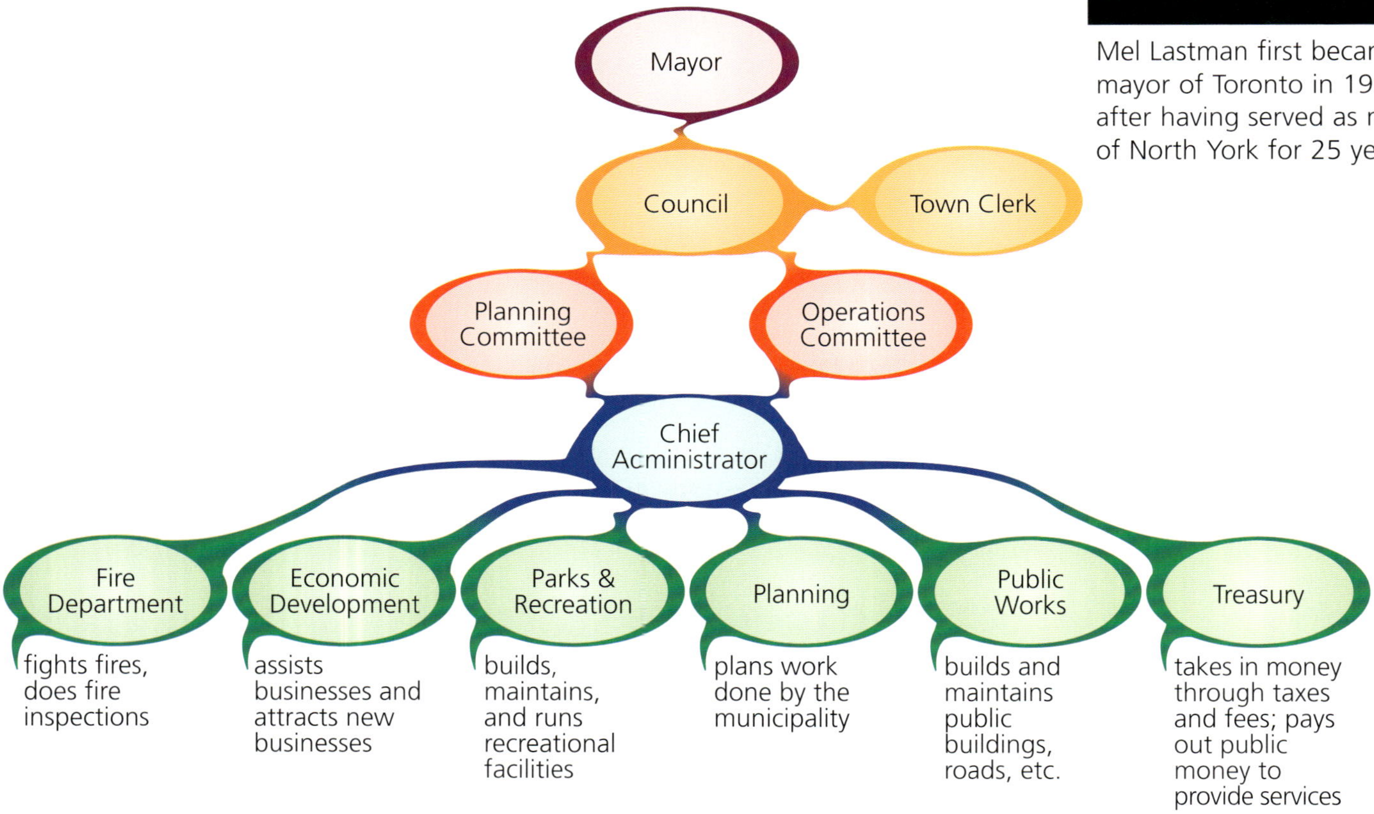

Services Provided by Municipalities

Municipalities provide many services within their boundaries. The council decides how much money to spend on each of the services they provide. The municipal government gets the money it needs from several sources:

- property taxes paid by the residents and businesses
- "user fees" charged for services such as swimming lessons at the Parks and Recreation Centres
- non-tax revenue such as parking fines
- money grants from the provincial government

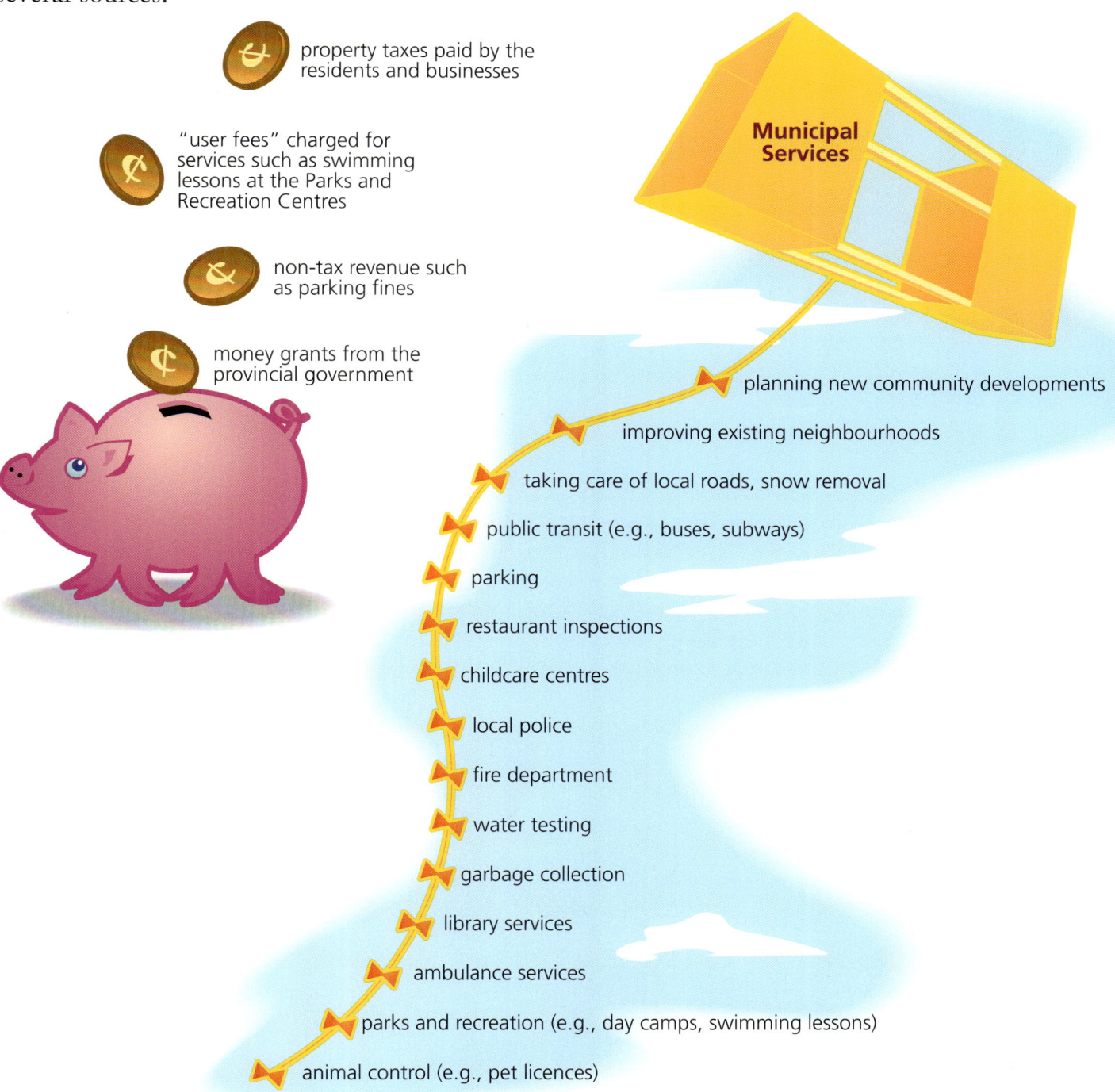

Municipal Services:
- planning new community developments
- improving existing neighbourhoods
- taking care of local roads, snow removal
- public transit (e.g., buses, subways)
- parking
- restaurant inspections
- childcare centres
- local police
- fire department
- water testing
- garbage collection
- library services
- ambulance services
- parks and recreation (e.g., day camps, swimming lessons)
- animal control (e.g., pet licences)

Do Discuss Discover

1. Why do you think municipalities take care of local roads and animal control?

Making a Shopping Bag Ad

Stores often advertise on special bags they use to package the goods they sell. These bags often have the store's logo or an image and a catchy phrase. When customers carry the bag around, they advertise the store to others. Some shopping bag ads also promote a public service such as recycling or the Food Bank.

You will need these materials to make your own shopping bag ad. The measurements in brackets apply to the sample net shown here. However, you may choose to use another net.

- piece of heavy mural paper or light-coloured packing paper (68 cm x 78 cm)
- large rectangular net (68 cm x 78 cm)
- large piece of newsprint or scrap paper
- scissors
- pencil and felt pens or paints
- glue, tape
- 2 strips of heavy paper or cord for handles (about 30 cm each)

1. Select a municipal service or event you would like to highlight or advertise.
2. Use the measurements shown on the sample to create your net or use another large rectangular net. Trace the net on heavy mural or packing paper. The net sample shown here leaves an opening at the top of the bag. If you use a different net, you may have to exclude the top panel to create an opening.
3. Cut out your net.
4. On scrap paper, sketch your ad design. Pay special attention to the placement of the picture or logo and the words. Remember, the bag will be seen from all sides.
5. Draw your complete design on your net. Use felt pens or paints to add bright colours.
6. Fold the tabs and glue your net together to make a shopping bag.
7. Glue or tape the two handles on the bag.
8. Display your bag.

Municipal Elections

In large cities across Canada, municipal elections are held every three or four years. In Ontario, they are held every three years on the second Monday in November.

All the voters in a municipality elect the head of council: the mayor or reeve. The person with the highest number of votes is elected.

There are two ways that councillors may be elected. In some municipalities, all the voters elect the councillors. Other municipalities may be divided into **wards**. Representatives are elected in each ward to sit on the council with the mayor. For example, the cities of Toronto, Regina, and Calgary all have councils made up of a mayor and ward representatives. Toronto city council has a mayor and 44 councillors who are ward representatives.

To participate in a municipal election, voters must be Canadian citizens and be 18 years of age or older. They must also live in or own property in the municipality.

Ross Rigney serves as Reeve in the Township of Minden Hills, Ontario.

Sandra Bussin, Municipal Councillor

"I've spent my whole life in the Beaches raising a family, creating jobs, and helping others. My experience has taught me how to get things done, bring people together, solve problems, be honest, and hold myself accountable for results. If we bring the same energy and focus that makes our streets safe and use it to improve public schools and public healthcare, this great city will be even better."

Sandra Bussin is presently serving a second term as city councillor for Beaches–East York. Before entering city politics, Sandra Bussin served as a public school trustee. She was also a high school teacher. Ms. Bussin also worked as a writer and researcher for members of the Ontario government.

Councillor Bussin has a long record of community service. She helps with fundraising for local needy families and the East General Hospital. She also volunteers with many social clubs and art foundations.

Do Discuss Discover

1. When will the next municipal election be held in your locality?

A Council's Role

The Municipal Act was passed by the Ontario provincial government. It describes the powers, duties, organization, and structure of municipalities in Ontario.

The job of a council is to listen to the voters and to make decisions about municipal planning and services. The council has the authority and responsibility to protect the health and safety of the residents. Councils set rules and regulations by passing written **bylaws**.

By comes from an Old Norse word that means town.

Making Bylaws

Someone in the municipality identifies a problem.

A councillor introduces a motion or a suggestion for a law.

Road signs remind people of bylaws that are in place for the well-being of residents.

The motion is discussed by the council members and may also be studied in a small group called a committee.

The whole council votes on the motion. If it is approved by a majority of the council members, it is carried or passed. The motion then becomes a bylaw.

Municipal governments plan and build community facilities such as this swimming pool in Windsor, Ontario.

http://cgii.gc.ca/muni-e.html

Visit this website and click on "Ontario" to find out about your municipal council.

Asking Questions to Gather Information

Asking good questions is an important research skill. Creating a list of questions can guide you to gather and classify the information you need on a topic.

1. Decide upon the purpose of your research; that is, decide what you want to know and what you intend to do with the information you gather.

2. Review the material you already know and check available resources to gain more understanding of the topic.

3. Write questions that will help you find interesting and insightful information about the topic.

   To gather factual information on a topic, ask questions that begin with *Who, What, Where,* and *When.*

   To gather more detailed information, beyond basic facts, use words such as *Explain, Why, How, Compare, Give an example, Describe, Would.*

4. Organize your questions in a logical order.

5. Decide which sources of information will likely provide answers to your questions. Some examples are library books and textbooks, the Internet, newspaper and magazine articles, and people. Often more than one source is needed to answer all questions.

6. Using your chosen sources, locate the information you need and write answers to your questions. Use your own words unless you are copying a direct quotation. (See page 11 about Getting Information from Quotations.) In this case, be sure to put quotation marks around the words. Keep a record of your sources of information, such as book titles and page numbers, in case you need to check details or find more information.

Do Discuss Discover

1. Re-read step 5 above. List five other sources of research information.
2. a) Use the suggestions above to prepare a set of questions for your local councillor. Find out about his or her working day, roles, and responsibilities.
   b) E-mail or write your councillor. Invite her/him to answer your questions.
   c) When you receive a response, use the information to write a narrative about how your councillor spends his or her day.

Provincial and Territorial Governments

In Canada, each province and territory has its own government and capital city. Provincial governments have three branches: the Executive Branch, the Legislative Branch, and the Judicial Branch.

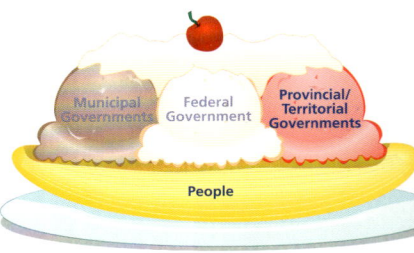

Structure of a Provincial Government

Legislative Branch

- Legislative (or National) Assembly (MPPs, MLAs, MNAs)

Executive Branch

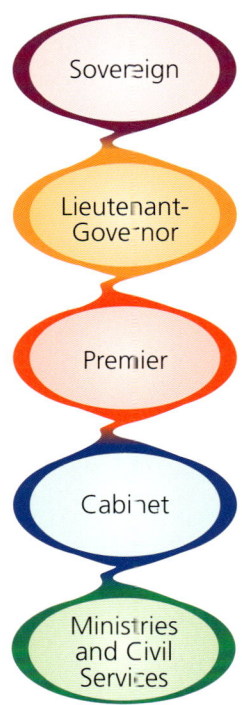

- Sovereign
- Lieutenant-Governor
- Premier
- Cabinet
- Ministries and Civil Services

Judicial Branch

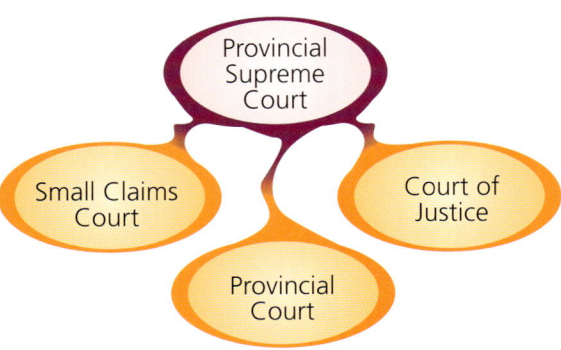

- Provincial Supreme Court
- Small Claims Court
- Court of Justice
- Provincial Court

In Ontario, the Provincial Legislature is located in Queen's Park, Toronto.

The legislative buildings of the Northwest Territories are located in the capital city of Yellowknife.

Provincial Government

In the Executive Branch, each provincial government has a **Lieutenant-Governor** who represents Queen Elizabeth II. The leader of the government is called a **Premier**. A Premier chooses a group of other elected members to be part of his or her **Cabinet**. Cabinet members help make decisions and are responsible for particular parts of the government's work.

In the Legislative Branch, the **Legislative Assembly**, or Legislature, is made up of all representatives who are elected. The Legislative Assembly discusses and makes laws. In Ontario, members of the Legislative Assembly are called Members of the Provincial Parliament (MPPs). In other provinces and territories, they are called Members of the Legislative Assembly (MLAs). In Quebec, the elected representatives are called Members of the National Assembly (MNAs).

In the Judicial Branch, the **judiciary** are the courts and judges who interpret and enforce the laws passed by the Legislative Assembly.

The Honourable James K. Bartleman (left), the first Aboriginal Lieutenant-Governor of Ontario, is congratulated on his appointment in 2002.

Territorial Government

Territorial governments are very similar to provincial governments. Each of the territories has a Legislative Assembly made up of representatives elected by the people in the territory. The leader of the Legislative Assembly is called the Premier or the Government Leader. The federal government appoints a Commissioner to work with the territorial government. This Commissioner is similar to a Lieutenant-Governor in a province.

Many types of cases are heard in provincial court, including those involving criminal offences, family law, and traffic violations.

Around the World

Canada has provinces and territories. Switzerland has cantons. Each canton controls its own education system and police force. Each canton also makes decisions about taxes.

Nunavut's MLAs meet in the Chamber of Nunavut's Legislative Assembly.

Do Discuss Discover

1. What is the name and title of your elected provincial representative?

Provincial Services

The provincial government has many duties and responsibilities for helping its citizens. The province provides funding for many services and institutions by transferring money to them. Most of the government's money comes from provincial taxes. Money is also transferred from the federal government to use for shared responsibilities such as medical services.

Provincial Elections

A provincial election is held whenever the Premier feels it is needed, but it must be within five years of the last election. The province is divided into electoral **ridings**. One representative is elected to the Legislature in each of these districts. To be eligible to vote on election day, a Canadian citizen must be 18 years or older and a resident of the electoral riding. In each riding, the person with the highest number of votes is elected Member of the Provincial Parliament (or MLA or MNA).

Most provincial **candidates**, people who choose to run for an elected position, belong to a **political party**. This is a group of people who share common political beliefs and ideas about what should be done for citizens. After an election, the political party that has the most candidates elected forms the provincial government. The leader of that political party becomes Premier.

Candidates' signs appear in all ridings during an election.

Making Laws

One of the key responsibilities of the Legislative Assembly is to make laws for its citizens.

Citizens are asking for a change in the speed limit on the provincial highways.

A member of the provincial parliament introduces a **bill** (a written idea for a law about an issue) in the Legislative Assembly.

Members of the Legislative Assembly study the bill. They vote to accept, change, or reject the bill.

If the bill is accepted, the Lieutenant-Governor or Commissioner signs it. It is now a law.

Do Discuss Discover

1. Create a chart in your notebook to compare municipal (review page 49) and provincial elections.

Aboriginal Self-Government

Aboriginal people are able to trace their systems of government back to the beginning of their oral history. Each group's culture, beliefs, and traditions are tied to their traditional lands. This has helped to shape their systems of government. The ability to control their lives and communities is important to the existences of Aboriginal groups.

As the country we know as Canada came into being, the right of **self-government** for most Aboriginal groups was limited or lost. Aboriginal groups' right to set up their own government instead of being part of a municipal, provincial, or territorial government has slowly been re-established since the late 1940s. Aboriginal leaders have struggled to help their people take their rightful place in Canada. They want to control their own lives and lands again. In 1995, the federal government began trying to negotiate practical ways of making Aboriginal self-government a reality.

In November 2001, Roberta Jamieson was elected Chief of the Six Nations in Ohsweken, Ontario.

Aboriginal peoples' goals for self-government include

- taking more responsibility for and control over decisions affecting their own lives and communities
- making their own laws and setting up their own services and programs such as education
- being more responsible to their own people for decisions they have made
- co-existing with their neighbouring communities and provinces.

Today Aboriginal governments are responsible for many services and programs in their communities, such as healthcare, housing and property rights, and adoption and child welfare.

In some Aboriginal communities today, self-government takes the form of a band council, which is similar to a municipal government.

Aboriginal governments look after such things as law making, language and culture, and police services.

Nunavut

"In the spring of 1979, Peter Ittinuar, our first Inuk Member of Parliament, stood up in the House of Commons and spoke Inuktitut. It may not have seemed like very much at the time, but to us it was another milestone in our epic journey."

— *John Amagoalik, Chief Commissioner of the Nunavut Implementation Commission. He served as the negotiator for the Inuit of Nunavut on the creation of Nunavut.*

Inuit drummers perform at the celebration in Iqaluit, Nunavut on April 1, 1999.

On April 1, 1999, a new territory called Nunavut was created by Canadian law. This territory was formerly part of the Northwest Territories. Nunavut is one-fifth of Canada's total land mass.

Nunavut means "Our Land" in Inuktitut, the language of the Inuit people. Nunavut has four major areas: Qikiqtaaluk, Kivalliq, High Arctic, and Kitikmeot. It has 28 communities spread over 350 000 square kilometres.

On Nunavut's flag, the colours blue and gold stand for the many gifts offered by the land, sea, and sky. Red is a symbol of Canada.

The territorial government of Nunavut is an elected Legislative Assembly with 19 MLAs. The people of the territory elect members every five years. The MLAs then select the Premier and Cabinet. Unlike the other provinces and territories, there are no political parties. All of the MLAs are involved in discussing and working out issues. Then, final decisions are based on a majority vote.

Iqaluit is the capital of Nunavut and also the largest community. Government departments and agencies are not clustered in the capital. The government decided to set up these departments and agencies throughout the territory. This allows the communities to share in the economic benefits these offices bring to the area. It also brings the government closer to all the people scattered throughout the territory.

To celebrate Canada's new territory, performers carry the flags of Canada's three territories and ten provinces.

Careers and Volunteers – Municipal

Karen Cooke, Aquatic Coordinator
Virginia Rubino, Aquatic Facilitator, Vaughan, Ontario

Hundreds of young people enjoy Dufferin Clark Community Pool every day. Both Karen Cooke and Virginia Rubino are making careers for themselves there. They began their careers in recreation when they were teenagers. Both became lifeguards and swim instructors and eventually became supervisors.

Karen decided that she wanted to learn more about her work. "I loved the recreation field ... I decided to go to college for Recreation Facility Management." Today she manages a crew of paid staff and volunteers. Together, they make sure that people in their community have a chance to enjoy the pool, learn to swim, or improve their skills. Pool safety is important to Karen. She makes sure that there are always trained lifeguards at her pool. She also ensures that pool users know how to enjoy the facility without getting hurt.

As facilitator, Virginia helps Karen with many of her responsibilities. She finds people who are interested in volunteering at the pool. She trains pool staff using the directions sent to her from the Ministry of Health. Virginia's work helps to make the pool a safe place to be. "This job is fun, interesting, and a great learning experience."

Cassandra Cairo, Pool Volunteer
Vaughan, Ontario

Cassandra's parents took her to swimming lessons when she was young. She loved to swim and looked forward to "pool days." She was also a good swimmer! She decided to take more lessons and hopes to become a swimming instructor and lifeguard in a few years. In the meantime, Cassandra volunteers at Dufferin Clark Community Pool whenever she can, usually during the summer months and on some weekends. She helps Karen and Virginia with the swim classes. "I really enjoy working with the children because I think swimming is an important skill that everyone should have. The children are so happy when they improve. That makes me happy, too."

Careers and Volunteers – Provincial/Territorial

Bernadette Norwegian, Intergovernmental Affairs Specialist, Yellowknife, Northwest Territories

Bernadette Norwegian is an intergovernmental affairs specialist, helping different governments work together to solve problems.

She works with the government of the Northwest Territories and various First Nations people to help them settle land claims. "Education and communication truly are the keys to acceptance and respect. Acceptance of what has been negotiated. Respect for the cultures that must learn to co-exist."

Bernadette Norwegian is also an artist. She is a respected painter who also writes poetry and song lyrics. Her writing has been published in the *Globe and Mail* newspaper.

My Native Voice

I have been away a long long time

My memories of the people they are my treasures

Old fathers fixing snowshoes

Old mothers working by the fire

Young dark eyes bright and beautiful

They are the jewels that glisten in the woods

I want to talk but I have been away so long.

– *by Bernadette Norwegian*

Roisin Hartnett, Legislative Page, Toronto, Ontario

Roisin Hartnett is a Grade 8 student at St. Matthew school in Oakville. She is also a legislative page at Queen's Park. Like all other pages, she delivers notes and bills to the 103 members in the Legislature. Unlike any legislative page before her, Roisin is blind.

"There are 103 seats ... in the House and I had to memorize all their names and where they sit." Roisin accomplished this in less than an hour. She and her guide dog, Penny, also learned how to move around the building. When Roisin and Penny first went to work in the Legislature, the room was full of people and television cameras were running. Penny happily guided Roisin through the rows of desks and around other people. The members admire Roisin's courage and appreciate her help. "She does a great job and we're all very proud of her," said Speaker Gary Carr.

Using Your Learning

Understanding Concepts

1. Make file cards for each of the Chapter 4 vocabulary words.

2. Using pages 47 and 54, design an organizer that identifies the services provided by the municipal and provincial governments.

3. In your notebook, create diagrams that illustrate the structure of your municipal and provincial governments. (Look back at pages 46 and 52.)

Developing Inquiry/Research and Communication Skills

4. Refer to the diagrams you created in question 3. Write the name of the current government leader on each one.

5. Visit the Indian and Northern Affairs kids' section at www.ainc-inac.gc.ca/ks.

   a) Click on "People" and then "Politicians" to learn about some Aboriginal politicians.

   b) Click on "History" and then "Dates in history after 1980." Create a timeline about ten recent events relating to Aboriginal self-government.

Developing Map/Globe Skills

6. a) Research which political party, if any, forms the government in each Canadian province and territory. Select a colour for each political party.

   b) On a map of Canada, colour each province and territory according to the political party that forms the government. Include all parts of a map.

Applying Concepts and Skills in Various Contexts

7. Create a series of questions you would like to ask the Premier about things happening at your school, in your community, or in your province. Hint: Look at page 54 for ideas.

In Your Scrapbook

1. Find an article in the newspaper about municipal or provincial government services. Try to find one with a picture.
2. Add it to your scrapbook.
3. Complete an organizer. (See page 17.) Add it to your scrapbook.
4. Include your narrative from Do Discuss Discover (DDD) question 2 on page 51 or another sample of your Chapter 4 work.

World Expo Link

Many people in your city would have to work together to host an exposition. In your group's World Exposition proposal, you will include people who participate in Canada's government as citizens and leaders.

1. As a class, discuss the challenges a city would face as thousands of visitors arrive for an exposition. For example, consider extra communication and transportation needs. How might such needs be met? Predict the roles that municipal and provincial levels of government might take.

2. You will showcase three people at your exposition. In this chapter, your group researches a volunteer. In upcoming chapters, you will do research on a civil servant and a federal government representative. Make an organizer like this one to record your notes.

	Volunteer	Civil Servant	Federal Government Representative
Name			
Role or position			
Sketch or picture			
Important dates			
Family			
Education			
Contributions			

3. Review with your project group what you have learned about volunteers in Chapters 2, 3, and 4.

4. Working with your group, find information about another volunteer and record it in your chart. Your information may be taken from books, the Internet, or personal connections.

Chapter 5
Federal Government: Executive Branch

The federal government of Canada has three parts to its structure. The Executive Branch includes the government leaders and the **civil service**. The civil service includes all of the government departments and their employees who carry out the jobs of government.

" We have an obligation to govern and to govern well and to govern every day we are in office. That is what we are elected for.

" The priorities we have set out are indeed the enduring priorities of Canadians: the health of our people, our environment, our economy, and the hopes of our children. "

– Jean Chrétien, Prime Minister

" In a democracy, government isn't something that a small group of people do to everybody else, it's not even something they do for everybody else, it should be something they do *with* everybody else. "

– Kim Campbell, former Prime Minister

Focus on Learning

In this chapter, you will learn about
- the structure of the federal government
- roles of the Sovereign, Governor General, Prime Minister, and Cabinet
- services provided by the federal government
- the work of the civil service

Vocabulary

- civil service
- Prime Minister
- Member of Parliament
- House of Commons
- head of state
- Governor General
- Royal Assent
- embassy
- ambassador
- diplomat

The Government of Canada

The federal government of Canada is made up of elected representatives from ridings all over Canada. They bring forward the people's concerns and wishes to the government in Ottawa, the national capital. All Canadian citizens have a right to vote for their representative by secret ballot.

The **Prime Minister** is the leader of the political party with the most elected **Members of Parliament** (MPs). MPs make laws and debate important issues. The Prime Minister chooses key members of the government for the Cabinet.

The Prime Minister assigns Cabinet Ministers to lead various government departments. Cabinet Ministers advise the Prime Minister on government issues. They also initiate laws and rules, especially dealing with money.

Cabinet Ministers are responsible to the **House of Commons**, which is made up of all the elected Members of Parliament. The House of Commons is responsible to the citizens of the country who elected the MPs.

Canada's original Parliament Buildings were completed in 1866. Upon Confederation, the buildings became a symbol of the new country and the place where federal government leaders would meet.

Structure of the Federal Government

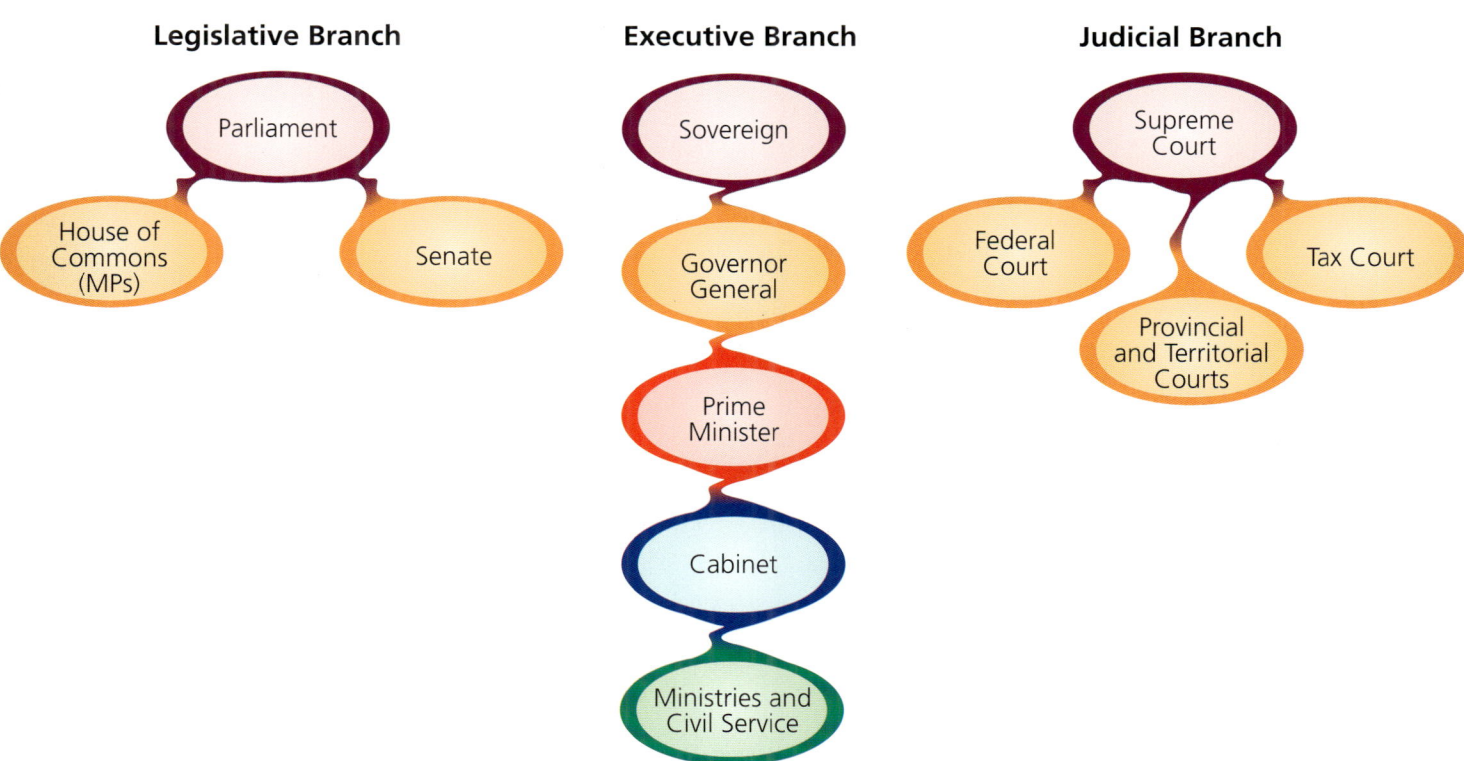

The Executive Branch

The Executive Branch is made up of the leaders of the government and the civil service.

Sovereign

Queen Elizabeth II is the formal **head of state** for Canada. A head of state is the person who officially represents the country. She/He is either a monarch or the leader of the ruling political party. In a democracy, the formal head of state is usually a ceremonial role. The Queen has no power to affect decisions in the Canadian government.

Governor General

The **Governor General** represents the Sovereign in Canada. The Prime Minister appoints the Governor General with the Queen's approval. The role of Governor General is mostly symbolic and ceremonial. She or he has no real power to affect what the government does or decides. The current Governor General is Her Excellency the Right Honourable Adrienne Clarkson.

Executive Branch

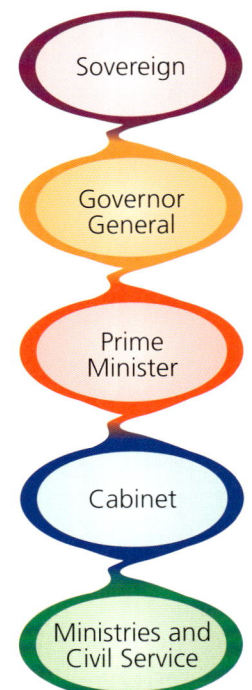

Duties of the Governor General

- officially open each session of Parliament by reading a speech prepared by the Prime Minister
- dissolve, or close, Parliament when an election is called
- give **Royal Assent** to laws passed in Parliament (approve them as the Queen's representative)
- direct the swearing-in of new Prime Ministers, the Chief Justices of Canada, and Cabinet Ministers
- be a symbol of Canada and promote Canada's national identity
- travel to foreign countries to celebrate Canada's accomplishments; welcome foreign leaders and representatives to Canada
- act as Commander-in-Chief of the Canadian Armed Forces
- reward excellence by presenting various honours, awards, medals, and decorations to outstanding Canadians
- participate in community events from coast to coast; visit hospitals, schools, fairs, and festivals; invite Canadians to come together and learn more about each other

Each Governor General has a personal coat of arms. Governor General Clarkson's coat of arms has a phoenix rising from flames. A maple leaf is shown inside the flames. Together, these parts symbolize her Chinese origin and the beginning of her new life as a Canadian.

The Governor General gives the Throne Speech on September 30, 2002, to open the session of Parliament.

The Governor General often visits military bases and welcomes troops when they come home from their tour of duty.

When government officials from other countries move to Canada, they must present their credentials to the Governor General before they can work.

The Governor General enjoys Canada Day celebrations with fellow Canadians.

Her Excellency the Right Honourable Adrienne Clarkson and His Excellency John Ralston Saul welcome Queen Elizabeth II and The Duke of Edinburgh to Iqaluit, Nunavut.

Around the World

In March 2003, citizens of Liechtenstein voted to give their monarch, Prince Hans Adam II, more power. He now has the right to dismiss governments, reject legislation, and approve the appointment of judges.

http://www.gg.ca

Search this website to find out about the different duties and responsibilities of the Governor General. In your notebook, create a job description for the position of Governor General.

Awards and Honours

The Canadian government has created numerous awards, medals, and certificates to honour Canadians who do outstanding things for our country. The awards presented by the Governor General recognize creativity, bravery, athletic and academic accomplishments, and community involvement.

The Order of Canada

The Order of Canada was created in 1967, the 100th anniversary of Confederation. The Order of Canada is given to recognize Canadians for extraordinary lifetime achievement and service to Canada or humanity. There are three levels: Member, Officer, and Companion (the highest level). These awards are presented by the Governor General.

The motto on the Order of Canada, "Desiderantes Meliorem Patriam," means *They Desire a Better Country*. The award recognizes Canadians for contributing their special work and talents to improve our way of life.

Sarah Anala, Member of the Order of Canada

Sarah Anala has demonstrated a deep concern for the well-being of Inuit, Mi'kmaq, and Maliseet peoples, offering her services as a counsellor to offenders and their families. She puts on many healing workshops throughout the Maritimes. She has sought to preserve her heritage and has forged new bonds of mutual understanding and respect between Aboriginal and non-Aboriginal peoples.

Bryan Adams, Member of the Order of Canada

Bryan Adams is one of Canada's most successful recording artists. He has received many music awards, including Male Artist of the Decade (1980s) from the Canadian Recording Industry Association.

He is also known for his work for famine relief, wildlife conservation, and human rights. He has been involved with causes such as Greenpeace and Save the Whales. He published two photographic books to support cancer research and has participated in charity concerts all over the world. He was awarded the Member of the Order of British Columbia and the Order of Canada in 1990. For his musical contributions and many volunteer efforts, Bryan was made an Officer of the Order of Canada in 1998.

Order of Merit of the Police Forces

This award was established in October 2000 to honour men and women of Canadian police forces. Recipients of this award have shown dedication beyond the call of duty.

Governor General's Academic Medal

In 1873, Lord Dufferin created the Governor General's Academic Medal to encourage academic excellence. Over the years, these medals have become the most prestigious awards students in Canadian schools can receive. They are awarded to students graduating with the highest average from high school, as well as from certain college or university programs.

The 2003 recipient of the Order of Merit of the Police Forces was Julian Fantino, Chief of Police for Toronto.

Elizabeth Gross, Recipient of the Governor General's Caring Canadian Award

Elizabeth Gross has reached out to her community in numerous ways. She helped set up Ottawa's drop-in and outreach centre called Centre 507. She also launched the Centretown Laundry Co-op, a laundry facility for low-income people. She organized meal programs to provide breakfasts and lunches to school children, and Christmas food hampers to families in need. She is also busy helping with church camps and Canadian Girls in Training. For her extraordinary contributions to her community, Elizabeth Gross received the Caring Canadian Award in 2003.

Ryan Victor Hreljac, Recipient of a Meritorious Service Decoration

In 1998, when he was six, Ryan Victor Hreljac from Kemptville, Ontario, decided to help African children. Many were dying because they did not have healthy, clean water. Ryan donated his allowance and money he earned doing chores. People heard about him and were inspired to help. They contributed over $60 000 to Ryan's project. The money went toward new well-building equipment in Uganda. Canada showed appreciation for his outstanding efforts when he was awarded a Meritorious Service Medal in 2002.

Do Discuss Discover

1. Imagine you are nominating one of your peers for the Governor General's Caring Canadian Award. Explain why you think this person is deserving of the award.

Prime Minister

The Prime Minister is the leader of the political party in power. He or she acts as the head of government. The current Prime Minister of Canada is Jean Chrétien.

Duties of the Prime Minister
- attend Cabinet meetings
- meet with visiting foreign officials
- answer questions in the House of Commons
- spend time helping the constituents that he or she represents
- represent Canada in international and world meetings, conferences, and negotiations
- meet with provincial Premiers to discuss issues

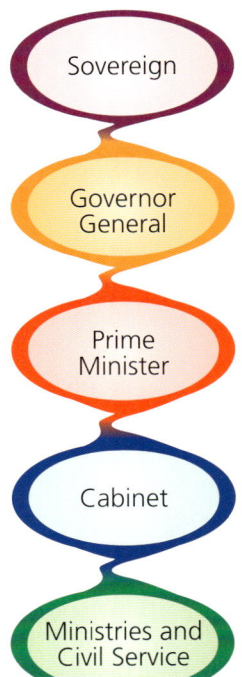
Executive Branch

Cabinet

The Prime Minister chooses Cabinet Ministers to help him/her discuss important issues affecting Canada. The Governor General officially appoints the Members of Parliament, who are chosen by the Prime Minister, to the Cabinet.

Duties of the Cabinet Ministers
- discuss important issues such as government spending, ideas for bills, and new policies, programs, and services
- take responsibility for a government department such as Foreign Affairs and International Trade or National Defence
- report to Parliament on her or his department's activities
- as a group, take responsibility for the government workings and its policies. Since this is a shared responsibility, they must all support a Cabinet decision in public.

Prime Minister Jean Chrétien responds to questions in the House of Commons.

At First Ministers' conferences, the Prime Minister and Premiers discuss matters of provincial and federal importance.

Pierre Pettigrew (centre) was appointed Minister for International Trade in 1999.

Services Provided by the Federal Government

The federal government provides services that apply to the whole country. These services are paid for by collecting fees and taxes from Canadians. The government decides how much money to spend on each of these services.

Federal Government Services

Agriculture
- food inspections
- food hazard alerts
- research

Culture
- Canadian Heritage
- the arts

Communication
- issue media licences

Citizenship and Immigration
- sets up rules for immigrants
- citizenship courts
- funds citizenship programs

Employment Insurance
- minimum wages
- parental leaves
- employment rights and responsibilities
- job training

Trade and Commerce
- interprovincial
- international
- trade agreements
- imports and exports

Justice and Attorney General
- federal courts
- advises the government on legal matters

Canada Pension Plan
- old age security

Transportation
- transcontinental highways (Hwy 1 or Trans Canada)
- railway safety issues
- pilot licencing
- marine safety
- civil aviation
- transportation of hazardous goods

Foreign Affairs
- passports
- embassies
- customs
- airport clearances
- trade with other countries

Health
- health promotions
- drug and cosmetic protection
- occupational health and safety
- medicine patents

Environment
- national parks
- community funding program
- Meteorological Service of Canada

Child and Family Benefits
- GST credits
- child tax benefit

Fisheries and Oceans
- fish habitat management

Canada Customs and Revenue
- forms and publications
- taxes

Finance
- Bank of Canada
- Royal Canadian Mint

Armed Services and Defence
- Reserves
- Canadian Forces College
- Military Police
- Air Cadets

Native Affairs and Northern Development
- treaties

Royal Canadian Mounted Police
- VIP security
- airport security
- Musical Ride

Canada Post
- stamps
- couriers

Civil Service

The civil service is the permanent, non-elected part of the government. It manages the government's programs and provides government services. The civil service also carries out the laws and rules made by the elected members of government.

The activities of the civil service are extremely varied. The web on this page shows just a few examples of the roles of federal civil servants and people who are paid to do jobs for the government.

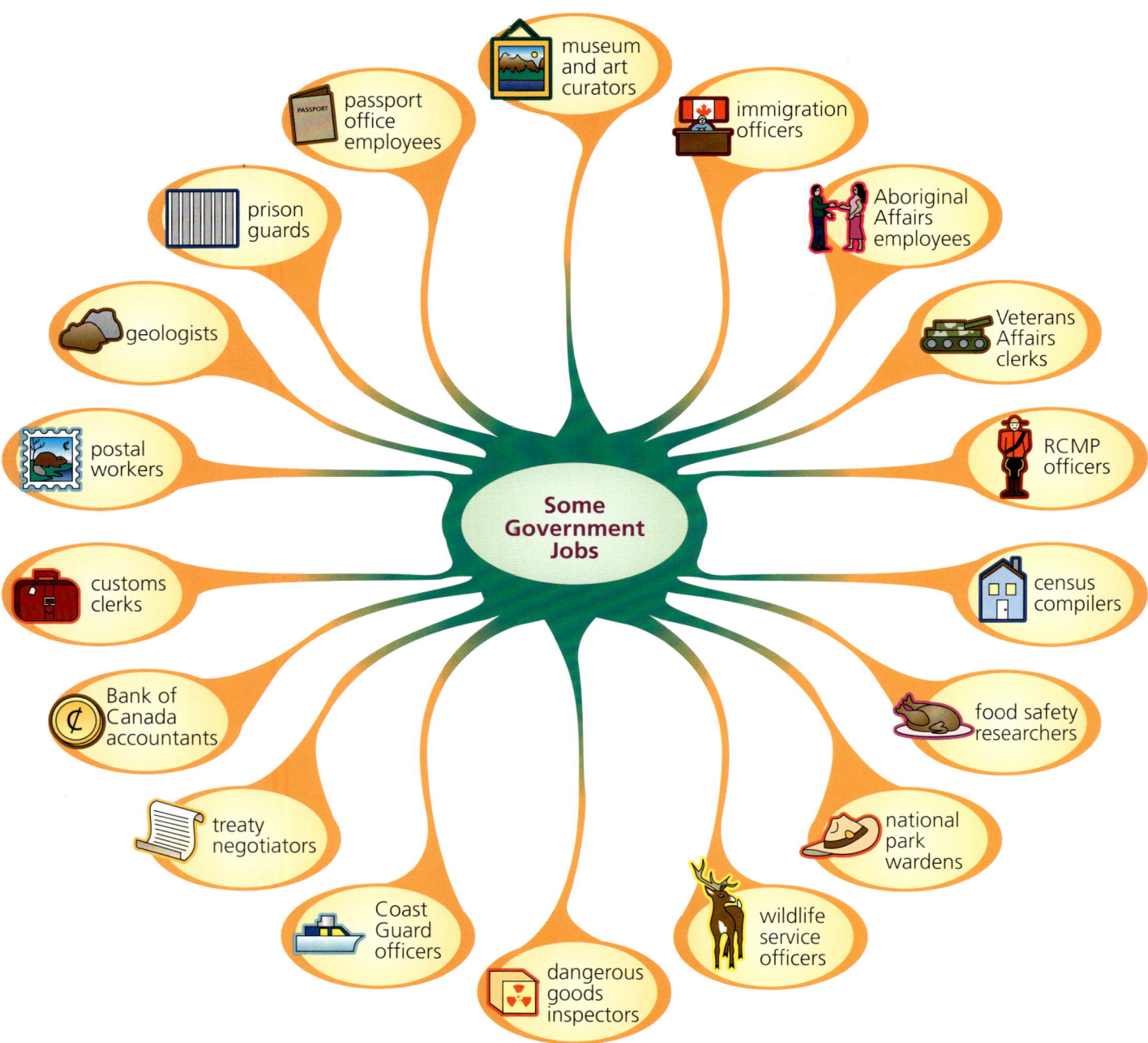

Careers

Dr. Sue Cosens, Whale Researcher

"When I first saw the Arctic, I felt I had gone back to the beginning of time. The Arctic is much more important to Canada than most people think it is."

Dr. Sue Cosens has been researching eastern Arctic bowhead whales since 1994. She camps out by the sea to study how well the whale population has recovered from near extinction. She examines the dangers these mammals encounter in the Arctic. After looking at the data, she makes recommendations to the government about how many whales can be safely hunted.

Tracey Vansickle, Foreign Service Officer

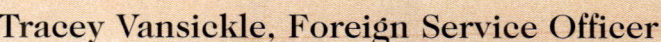

"You have to be people-oriented to do this job, to get people to tell you their stories. If you can't get along with people, you can't do this job."

Tracey Vansickle is off work early today—it's only 8 p.m. In spite of her long day, she is full of energy as she talks about her work with refugees in the largest refugee camp in Macedonia. The refugee camp has held up to 30 000 refugees from war-torn Bosnia.

Tracey Vansickle interviews these refugees to see if Canada will be willing to offer them a home. For example, in the camp there is a doctor who wants to come to Canada. He will have to take all his exams again to qualify as a doctor in Canada, but he is determined to make a better life for his family.

"This is an opportunity to go in and help people, to do something that's good."

Glen Peers, Park Warden, Parks Canada, Banff, Alberta

"When I look back at my career with Parks, I hope I'll be able to say I did my part to maintain one of this country's most precious natural resources."

As Senior Park Warden, one of Glen Peers' responsibilities is to keep the animals safe from humans and vice versa. For example, during the summer, elk come into Banff to graze on the lawns. He deals with about 500 elk incidents every year.

Mr. Peers is a Montrealer who came to Banff to work as a lifeguard one summer while in college. He says he stumbled into his life work there. He gets paid for doing something he likes and enjoys having an outdoor life.

The RCMP

The Royal Canadian Mounted Police is Canada's national police force. The main purpose of the RCMP is to enforce the laws passed by Parliament.

The RCMP has many responsibilities such as policing Canada's borders and the Arctic region, providing police air and marine services, and posting officers in Canadian embassies around the world. They also provide police services to all of Canada's provinces and territories, and to over 200 municipalities. To assist them in their policing work, they have special branches, such as a forensic laboratory, to help them with crime detection.

The RCMP has also been asked by Parliament to take part in international police duties. Since 1989, more than 1200 police officers from the RCMP and 28 provincial and municipal Canadian police forces have served on international peacekeeping or peace support missions around the world.

The RCMP provides police service across Canada.

Peacekeeping Service Medals are presented to ten police officers by the Governor General in September 2000.

The red uniform of the RCMP is worn for official duties and ceremonies such as the opening of Parliament. It is recognized worldwide.

http://www.rcmp-grc.gc.ca/news/2000/nr-00-16.htm

Visit this website to learn about the many places around the world where RCMP officers have performed peacekeeping duty.

Do Discuss Discover

1. The RCMP is a symbol of Canada.
   a) Discuss with a partner the meaning of this symbol. In your notebook, write a paragraph about this Canadian symbol.
   b) Create a list identifying where you might see an officer of the RCMP.

Careers

Dan Polegato, RCMP Blacksmith

While it may seem like fun to those who see the show, the life of a horse in the Musical Ride is not an easy one. Just ask Dan Polegato, the Musical Ride's blacksmith for almost 20 years.

"The average rider may ride their horse for a half hour after work. Here, our horses work an hour and a half in the morning alone and almost three to four hours every day."

Dan is sensitive to the problems this kind of activity can have on a horse. "Like a car, the more kilometres you put on a horse the more problems begin to arise."

Dan travels with the Musical Ride every second year. He prepares for anything that the horses might need as they travel the country. "I make up extra shoes before we leave and bring along as much equipment as I can. You might not find what you need in some small towns we visit."

Despite the travel, the hard work, and the occasional temperamental horse, Dan says he wouldn't change jobs with anyone. "Not when you see the look on people's faces when I tell them I'm with the RCMP Musical Ride."

Embassies

There is a little piece of Canada in most countries in the world. This little piece of Canada is called an **embassy**. The staff at Canadian embassies assist Canadians while they are outside Canada, promote Canadian trade and goods produced in Canada, and encourage cultural exchanges between Canada and other countries.

An embassy is the residence of the Canadian **Ambassador** to that country. Ambassadors are part of the federal government Department of Foreign Affairs and International Trade. The Prime Minister appoints them to their posts.

Most ambassadors are career **diplomats**, but they can be former politicians. A diplomat works for a government's foreign service and conducts official negotiations with other countries. Some examples of negotiations are settling disagreements between countries, making special arrangements, or doing business.

A Canadian embassy is located in Washington, D.C., the capital of the United States.

Stephen Lewis

From 1984 to 1988, Stephen Lewis was the Canadian Ambassador to the United Nations. There he presented the Canadian view on many world problems. He also chaired the first international conference on climate change and global warming.

In 1990, Stephen Lewis was appointed as Special Representative for UNICEF. In that job, he travelled and spoke about the rights and needs of children. He served as the Deputy Executive Director of UNICEF at its world headquarters in New York from 1995 to 1999.

In 2001, the Secretary-General of the United Nations appointed Stephen Lewis to work in the fight against HIV/AIDS in Africa. For his contributions to Canada and the world, he was named a recipient of the Companion of the Order of Canada in 2003.

Do Discuss Discover

1. Which of the jobs on pages 70 to 74 would you like to have? Write a personal reflection giving your reasons for choosing that job.
2. Why might travelling Canadians need the help of an embassy?

Using Your Learning

Understanding Concepts

1. Make file cards for each of the Chapter 5 vocabulary words.
2. Begin a diagram that illustrates the structure of the federal government. Show the Executive Branch. You may want to add pictures. You will complete the diagram in Chapter 6.

Developing Inquiry/Research and Communication Skills

3. Identify the names of five current federal Cabinet Ministers. For what government department is each responsible?
4. If you could meet the Governor General, what five questions would you ask about her/his role in government?

Applying Concepts and Skills in Various Contexts

5. a) Think of concerns you have about issues in your community or country. Which ones are the responsibility of the federal government?

   b) Write a letter asking the Prime Minister to respond to your concerns.

6. Create an advertisement for one of the jobs in the civil service. Remember to include the traits that are most suitable for the job.

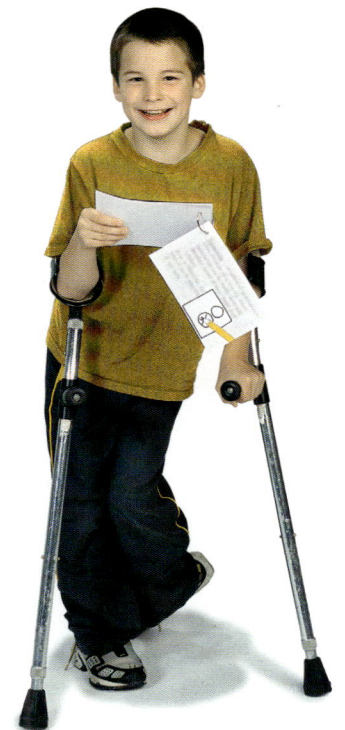

In Your Scrapbook

1. To learn about how your federal government is working for you, complete one of these and add it to your scrapbook:

   a) Look through the Government of Canada section in your telephone directory. Write down five services listed there.

   b) Find a letter to the editor in your local or national newspaper.

2. Complete an organizer. (See page 17.) Add it to your scrapbook.
3. Add your personal reflection from DDD question 1 on page 74 or another sample of your Chapter 5 work.

World Expo Link

1. Review the information in Chapter 5 about civil servants. Discuss as a class the many services they provide.
2. With your project group, do research to learn about a civil servant.
3. Record the information in the chart you started in Chapter 4. (See page 61.)

Chapter 6
Federal Government: Legislative and Judicial Branches

The Legislative Branch of the federal government is Canada's Parliament. Its two parts, the House of Commons and the Senate, are responsible for making laws. The Judicial Branch of the federal government includes the courts and judges who enforce the laws of Canada.

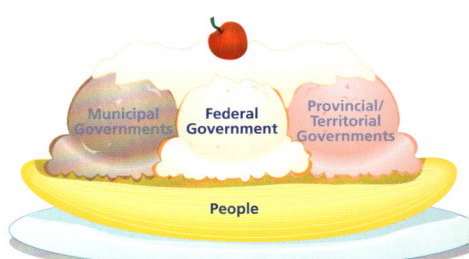

" The role of the Official Opposition in a democracy is to check government proposals and to provide alternatives. By playing this role, the opposition promotes public discussion about important issues. "

– *Stephen Harper, Leader of the Canadian Alliance, the Official Opposition*

" I encourage all young Canadians to take part in public life. Public service is an opportunity open to each of us to help shape the communities in which we live and the country of which we are so proud. It is a privilege to serve my community as a Member of Parliament and in the Government of Canada as a Cabinet Minister. "

– *Anne McClelland, MP and Minister of Health*

" The justice system of Canada is very much admired in this world. Members of the Supreme Court and judges and lawyers receive great numbers of invitations to visit other countries, and judges from other countries come here. Our system of justice is a very special feature of this country. "

– *Mr. Justice (Honourable) Frank Iacobucci*

Focus on Learning

In this chapter, you will learn about
- the House of Commons and MPs
- the opening of Parliament
- interviewing
- the Senate and Senators
- how a bill becomes law
- the Judicial Branch of government

Vocabulary

- constituency
- Speaker of the House
- impartial
- Throne Speech
- Senate
- independent judiciary
- Supreme Court
- appeal

House of Commons

The House of Commons is the major law-making body in Canada's Parliament. There are 301 elected Members of Parliament (MPs) who have seats in the House of Commons. Members of Parliament are men and women who are elected by the citizens of their **constituencies** across Canada. Constituencies are also known as ridings or electoral districts.

Seats in the House of Commons are distributed roughly in proportion to the population of the various provinces or territories. The more people in a province, the more Members it has in the House of Commons.

After every general election, the Members of Parliament elect a **Speaker of the House** from among the MPs by secret ballot. The Speaker's main responsibility is to make sure everyone respects the rules and traditions of Parliament. The Speaker must apply the rules equally to all Members. He or she must be **impartial** and not take sides.

Legislative Branch

Duties of MPs
- debate and vote on bills
- make important decisions about spending public money and imposing taxes
- represent the views of their constituents
- discuss national issues
- call on the government to explain its actions

The Honourable Peter Milliken was elected by fellow MPs as Speaker of the House of Commons in 2001.

Distribution of House of Commons Seats (2003)

Area	Population	Seats
Alberta	3 113 600	26
British Columbia	4 141 300	34
Manitoba	1 150 800	14
New Brunswick	756 700	10
Newfoundland	531 600	7
Northwest Territories	41 400	1
Nova Scotia	944 800	11
Nunavut	28 700	1
Ontario	12 068 300	103
Prince Edward Island	139 900	4
Quebec	7 455 200	75
Saskatchewan	1 011 800	14
Yukon Territory	29 900	1
Total	31 414 000	301

Statistics Canada

Do Discuss Discover

1. Create a chart of the provinces and territories arranged in order from fewest to most seats.
2. Design a graph to show the distribution of seats in the House of Commons.

The Opening of Parliament

The opening of Parliament is full of symbols and ceremony that were adopted from the British Parliament.

The Gentleman Usher of the Black Rod enters the House of Commons and asks for the presence of the Members of Parliament in the Senate Chamber. This is because traditionally, the Governor General and Senators are not allowed to enter the House of Commons. The Usher leads the MPs to the front entrance of the Senate Chamber. The Sergeant-at-Arms of the House of Commons carries the parliamentary mace and goes with them.

A Look Inside the House of Commons

1. Speaker
2. Pages
3. Government Members
4. Opposition Members
5. Prime Minister
6. Leader of the Official Opposition
7. Leader of the Second-Largest Party in Opposition
8. Clerk and Table Officers
9. Mace
10. Hansard Reporters (record the proceedings)
11. Sergeant-at-Arms
12. Interpreters
13. Press Gallery
14. Public Gallery
15. TV Cameras

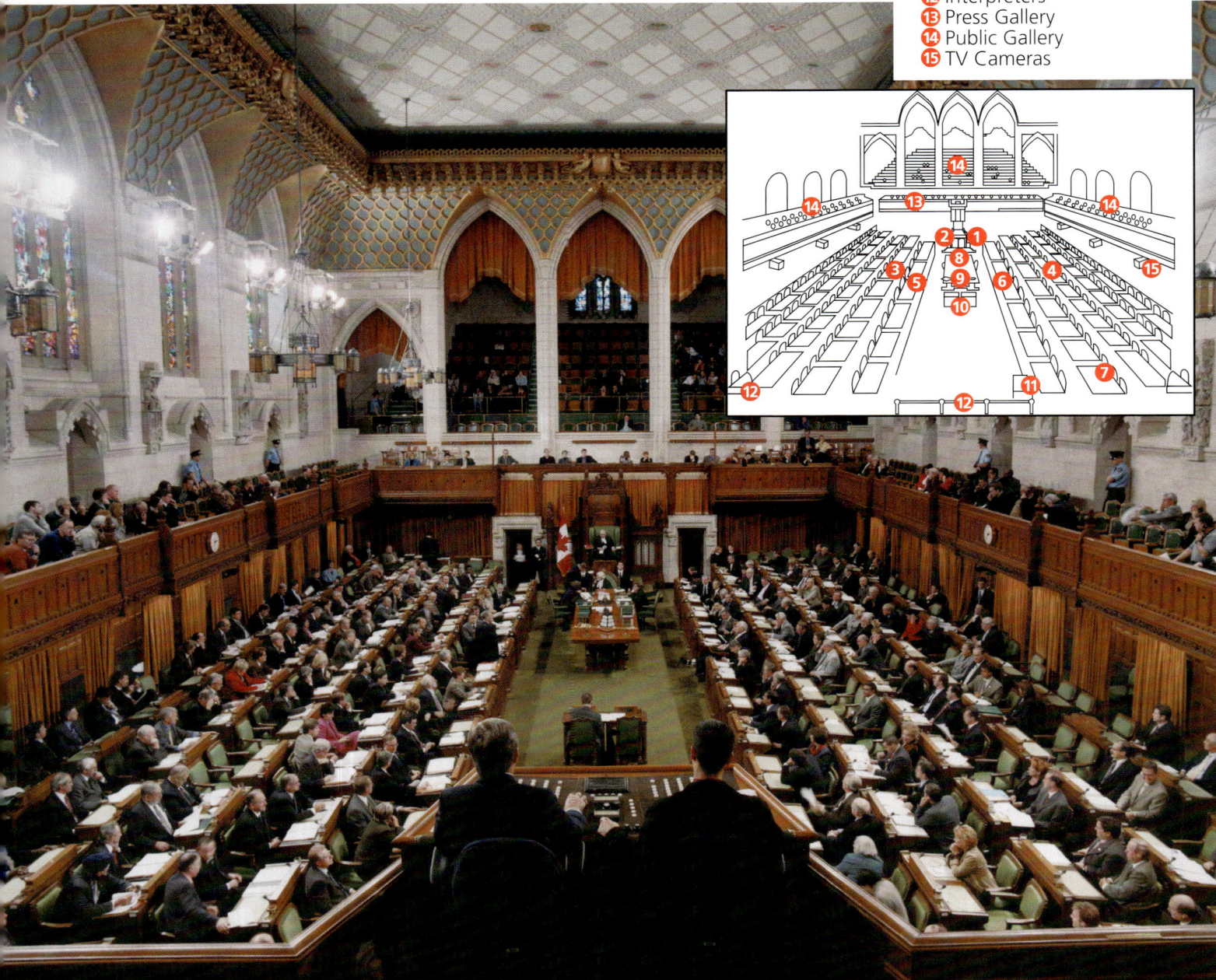

The Governor General delivers the speech in the Senate Chamber. She or he sits on a throne made of oak and red velour. The MPs listen to the speech outside the front entrance of the Senate Chamber. The Prime Minister is the only Member of Parliament inside the Senate Chamber during the speech.

The Prime Minister writes the **Throne Speech** that is read by the Governor General at the opening of Parliament. The speech outlines the government's main objectives for the upcoming session of Parliament. It can be described as the government's plan of action for the session.

Speaker's Chair

The Speaker's Chair sits on a raised platform called a dais. The original Speaker's Chair burned in the fire of 1916. The present chair was a gift to Canada given by England on May 20, 1921.

Parliamentary Mace

In medieval times, a mace was a weapon used to defend the monarch. Today it symbolizes the authority the monarch has given to the House of Commons to meet and decide on the laws that govern the country.

The Speaker's Chair is an exact replica of the chair that is found in the British House of Commons.

The parliamentary mace, or the Speaker's Mace, is present at all sittings of the House of Commons. The Sergeant-at-Arms carries the mace into the Chamber to begin a working day.

The fire of 1916 destroyed the original mace. First, a wooden replacement was made. In 1917, the Sheriffs of London gave Canada a new golden mace. The wooden mace is used each year on February 3 to remember the date of the devastating fire.

When the Speaker sits in the Speaker's Chair, the mace is placed on the table to show that the House of Commons is in session.

Do Discuss Discover

1. In your notebook, create an agenda for the opening of Parliament. Make sure you include all the people and symbols involved.

Report from Tony Rimko, a Parliamentary Page

September 2002

I have been in Ottawa since mid-August. That is when I began the intense training to become a House of Commons parliamentary page. It was hard work, but it was also fun. I enjoyed getting to know the other 39 parliamentary pages.

When my Grade 8 class visited Ottawa, our teacher told us about this opportunity for all young Canadians. I decided then that I wanted to become a page when I was old enough.

During high school, I studied hard because I had to maintain an average of 80% or over to qualify. I took part in the school's debating club, basketball team, and swim team. I especially enjoyed my Grade 10 Civics Course where I learned all about the workings of government. I volunteered at my MP's constituency office during the last federal election. These activities all helped me prepare for becoming a parliamentary page.

I submitted my application in the fall of my Grade 12 year. I had to include proof I was a Canadian citizen or a permanent resident, a copy of my high school marks, and proof that the University of Ottawa had accepted me into their Political Science course. I also had to demonstrate that I could speak in both official languages at a superior level. My French teacher and principal wrote letters of reference for me.

I also had to write a 500-word essay describing my qualities, talents, and interests. In the essay, I described how I would make a positive contribution to the page programme and how I would benefit from being part of it.

During the orientation for the programme, I was introduced to my job responsibilities and to the key people in Ottawa. My duties include running messages to MPs in the House of Commons, fetching glasses of water, and occasionally performing ceremonial duties with the House of Commons Speaker when foreign dignitaries visit. One duty I am going to enjoy is meeting with high school groups to describe my experience as a parliamentary page.

I will enjoy this year in Ottawa. I feel like I am an eyewitness to modern Canadian history, seeing our nation's decision-makers at work. I will experience directly what others only read about in their daily newspapers.

Making a Mural

Work as a class to create a mural of the House of Commons.

You will need
- mural paper
- pencils and erasers, rulers
- paints, felt pens, crayons

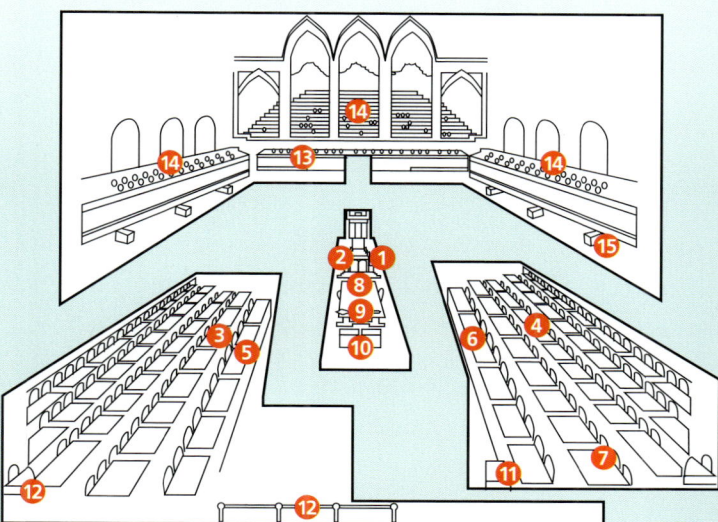

1. Examine the pictures of the House of Commons found in this textbook. You may wish to do additional research on the Internet for the people and symbols that are part of the workings of the House of Commons.

2. Form four groups and divide the mural into four sections. Each group is responsible for a section of the mural. (A suggestion for the division of the mural is shown here.)

3. On mural paper, sketch your section of the House of Commons with your group. Include all of the parts shown in your section on page 78. Use a different colour to label each of the different parts. Include a legend.

   Remember: Be careful in your work. All four sections must properly fit together.

4. Combine the four sections of the mural and display it in a prominent place in the classroom.

5. On a copy of the House of Commons provided by your teacher, colour and label the different parts. Use the mural as your reference.

Report from Peter Adams, Member of Parliament for Peterborough, Ontario

I have been a Member of Parliament since 1993. I work hard to bring the needs and opinions of the people in my community to the government's attention. I also help to make decisions that affect the whole country. Whether I am in Ottawa or in my home riding, my days are always busy.

When I am in Peterborough, I usually work in my constituency office. People meet me there to ask questions and to discuss their concerns. I receive many invitations to events around Peterborough. For example, I might be invited to a high school graduation ceremony. There are helpers working at my constituency office who look after people when I am not there.

Members of Parliament must be present in Ottawa whenever the House sits, or meets. That usually happens 130 days out of the year. Luckily, I can drive to the capital from Peterborough in a few hours.

When I am in Ottawa, I often work as part of a parliamentary committee. These committees are groups of Members of Parliament who work together to examine a problem. For example, a committee might study fishing. How many fish should the government let people catch? Committees talk to experts and also to the public. They read about the problem. The committees then write reports that inform other Members about the problem.

The most important work in Ottawa is done in the House of Commons. Each session begins with ringing bells that summon Members. The Sergeant-at-Arms carries the mace into the House. The Speaker and the clerks follow the Sergeant. The Speaker leads in a short prayer, and then calls the House to order. Some may say that the ceremony is old fashioned, but it helps to remind us that we do important work in Ottawa.

There are 301 Members in the House. Imagine how confused it could become if we all spoke at once! There are rules that determine when we can talk. Any Member can speak about any issue, but only for one minute! Members in the Opposition also question the government about its work.

Since my election, I feel I have brought positive changes to my community. This makes all the hard work worthwhile.

Do Discuss Discover

1. Which part of an MP's role do you think is the most important? Why?

Interviewing

An interview is a conversation conducted to gather information. You can interview someone in person or over the telephone. The information can be written down and, with the person's permission, you can record it on audio or videotape. The following guide can be used to plan, set up, and conduct an interview.

1. **Plan the interview:**
   - Determine the purpose of the interview.
   - Contact the person you wish to interview (the interviewee) by sending a letter or calling him/her on the telephone.
   - Introduce yourself to the interviewee and state your purpose. Ask permission to record the interview on audio or videotape.

2. **Prepare for the interview:**
   - Review page 51, Asking Questions to Gather Information.
   - Gather background information by researching your topic.
   - Design five good questions. Always keep your purpose in mind.
   - Test your equipment and practise using it before the interview.
   - Sequence the questions from general to specific and practise them.
   - Call to confirm the time and place for the interview.

3. **Conduct the interview:**
   - Arrive in plenty of time to choose a quiet place to conduct the interview and set up.
   - Do not rush or interrupt the interviewee. You are there to listen and probe for information.
   - Try to keep eye contact and use encouraging facial expressions.
   - Take notes of the key points.
   - Ask follow-up questions if you need clarification on a question.
   - Thank the interviewee and tidy up the area you used.

4. **Write out the interview and conclude the process:**
   - While the interview is still fresh in your mind, write the words from the tape onto paper. Include both the questions and the answers.
   - Send a note of thanks and a copy of the written notes to the interviewee.
   - Write a summary of what you learned during the interview.

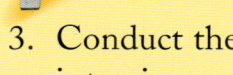

Do Discuss Discover

1. Review the skills above and then interview a family or community member about the most important roles of the federal government.

The Senate

The **Senate** is the other part of Parliament. Along with the House of Commons, the Senate participates in making laws for all of Canada. Senators are not elected like MPs. Its members are chosen by the Prime Minister and appointed by the Governor General.

Senators come from different political parties, different parts of the country, and all backgrounds. Many Senators have previous experience in municipal, provincial, and federal government. A few are chosen because they are greatly respected in their communities for the contributions they have made.

Senators reflect Canada's multicultural society. There are English- and French-speaking Senators whose roots can be traced to all parts of the world, as well as Senators who are Aboriginal leaders. Senators can hold office until they are 75 years old or until they miss two consecutive sessions of Parliament. Today 35% of the Senators are women.

Senators can introduce, change, and reject bills. A bill is a document that proposes that something become law. Most bills are introduced by MPs in the House of Commons while Parliament is in session. No bill becomes law unless it is passed by both the House of Commons and the Senate.

Number of Senators (2003)

Alberta	6
British Columbia	6
Manitoba	6
New Brunswick	10
Newfoundland	6
Northwest Territories	1
Nova Scotia	10
Nunavut	1
Ontario	24
Prince Edward Island	4
Quebec	24
Saskatchewan	6
Yukon Territory	1
Total	**105**

Parliament of Canada

Duties of the Senators

- work in committees
- study bills carefully
- listen to representatives of groups that will be most affected by a bill becoming law
- write reports for Parliament on important public problems such as poverty, land use, and Canada's relations with our trading partners

Senator Thelma Chalifoux, Alberta

In 1997, Thelma Chalifoux became the first Aboriginal woman to be appointed to the Senate and the first Métis woman in Parliament. She has dedicated her life to her community, bringing about greater understanding between cultures.

A Bill Becomes Law

Issue
1. An issue is identified. For example, should the voting age be lowered to 16?

Bill Introduced
2. A Member of Parliament introduces a bill to address the issue.

Committee
3. The bill is then sent to a committee of MPs who will study it.

Readings/Debate/Final Vote
4. When the bill returns from the committee, it is debated in the House of Commons in the first reading. A vote is taken. If passed, it goes to a second reading and another vote. If passed, it goes to a third reading. It is discussed and debated again, and a final vote is taken. If it passes, it goes to the Senate for review.

Senate Review/Vote
5. When the House of Commons approves the bill, it goes to the Senate for review. There are also three readings in the Senate. The Senate votes to accept, reject, or change it. After the third reading, a final vote is taken. If passed, the bill goes forward for Royal Assent.

Royal Assent
6. After both Houses approve the bill, it is signed by the Governor General and proclaimed a new law.

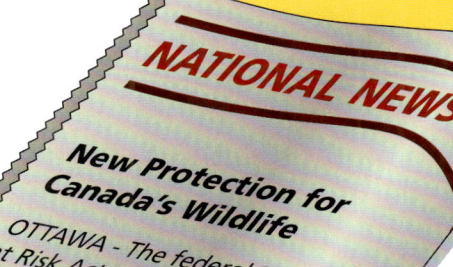

NATIONAL NEWS

New Protection for Canada's Wildlife

OTTAWA - The federal Species at Risk Act was given Royal Assent today. Bill C-5, first introduced in the House of Commons in 2001, will come into force in 2003. The Act is designed to protect endangered species from extinction and

Do Discuss Discover

1. a) In a small group, discuss issues that are important to you. Take a position on an issue that your group is willing to support.

   b) Write a list of reasons why your whole class should support this position. Present these reasons to the class.

Judicial Branch

The Judicial Branch is part of the federal government, but its judges and courts are completely independent of the Legislative and Executive Branches. Having an **independent judiciary** means the government cannot force judges to make decisions the government wants. Judges discuss, interpret, and rule on laws without the influence of the rest of government.

The Supreme Court

The **Supreme Court** of Canada is part of the federal government's Judicial Branch.

The Supreme Court was established by an Act of Parliament in 1875. It is the highest court in Canada. It is made up of nine judges, three of whom come from Quebec. The Governor General makes new appointments to the Supreme Court based on recommendations from the Cabinet. Supreme Court Justices may hold office until they are 75 years old.

Judicial Branch

- Supreme Court
- Federal Court
- Tax Court
- Provincial and Territorial Courts

Around the World

Both Canada and the United States have democratic governments. Even so, there are some differences. In the United States, Senators are elected, not appointed as they are in Canada. The President of the United States nominates Supreme Court Justices. Justices are officially appointed if the Senate consents.

Duties of the Supreme Court

- discuss, interpret, and rule on laws and legal issues for all of Canada
- hear criminal and civil cases referred by the Provincial and Territorial Courts, as well as the Federal Court
- act as the highest court of **appeal** in the country. An appeal is a request to have a higher court review a decision made by a lower court.
- interpret the Canadian Constitution and make final decisions on Constitutional questions. For example, the Supreme Court defines the limits of provincial and federal powers.

Everyone in Canada is subject to the law—including the Prime Minister and Parliament.

Supreme Court Justices hear cases in the Main Courtroom, located in the centre of the Supreme Court Building in Ottawa.

Interview with a Supreme Court Judge
Mr. Justice (Honourable) Frank Iacobucci

Wednesday, July 23, 2002

Interviewers Mary Cairo and Luci Soncin: Did you always want to be a lawyer as you were growing up?

Mr. Justice Iacobucci: I got the idea of becoming a lawyer from my elementary school principal. At graduation, he said a few words about me. He described me as a talker and said that as a lawyer, I could best use my talents.

Interviewers: Who were your role models as you were growing up?

Mr. Justice Iacobucci: I was blessed in my life with a number of role models. My mentors were my schoolteachers, athletic coaches, and my parents. As I got older, I was influenced by Mr. Angelo Branca, a well-known lawyer in British Columbia, later appointed to the British Columbia Court of Appeal. He was a very successful lawyer of Italian-Canadian heritage.

Interviewers: How were your coaches your mentors?

Mr. Justice Iacobucci: My coaches encouraged me to learn lessons about life from sports. My parents were immigrants, so I was brought up on the poor side of town. There was much opportunity to get into trouble. Sports kept me on the right path. Some of the lessons I learned were that there was always someone better than you, that you knew you were going to lose at some point, and the important thing was how you lost. You had to be able to bounce back. You also had to get along with your teammates.

Interviewers: What do you consider your most important duty as a Supreme Court Judge?

Mr. Justice Iacobucci: The oath of office is to apply and define the law to the best of our ability. We are judges—we are not politicians. Our role is to interpret and apply the law. It is my job description, but it's also the most important part of what I do.

Interviewers: What is the most challenging part of your job?

Mr. Justice Iacobucci: Well, there are many challenges in the job. First of all, the questions presented are very challenging questions. They are questions of difficulty. To some extent, we deal with many of society's issues. We have examined issues of equality, discrimination, criminal process, social questions, and a whole host of other concerns.

Interviewers: How are judges selected to hear a particular case?

Mr. Justice Iacobucci: Although every Supreme Court Judge has the right to sit on every case, the Chief Justice actually assigns judges to hear cases. We sit in groups of nine, seven, or five.

Interviewers: How do you prepare for a case?

Mr. Justice Iacobucci: There's a fair amount of preparation. Cases only come here after other courts in the system have already looked at them. We look at the judgement of those courts, and we look at arguments the parties have put forward. We would look at the precedents [previous cases or legal decisions], and sometimes there would be an article to read. I have three law clerks who prepare a summary of previous lower court decisions, arguments presented, and an analysis of the law. I use that as a tool to prepare, then I add my own impressions. It is time-consuming, but when I go in to hear a case, I believe I'm very well prepared.

Interviewers: So the hearing itself is just to get further clarification?

Mr. Justice Iacobucci: Exactly. It is for further clarification of what the lawyers want to emphasize and what the judges want to emphasize or explore. The hearing is to increase the judges' understanding.

Interviewers: When does the Supreme Court hear cases?

Mr. Justice Iacobucci: The sitting starts at the end of September or early October and closes the end of June. We don't sit during July and August, but there's lots of work to do writing judgements.

Interviewers: What important message do you want students to have about our government?

Mr. Justice Iacobucci: First, I would encourage them to learn about their government and how Canada is governed because there may be some misunderstandings out there. I don't think they get the right information or the right impression just by reading the newspapers. So, learn about your government.

Second, I'd want them to know that Canada is a leader in government. They should appreciate how special the Canadian system of government is, with its three branches: Executive, Legislative, and Judicial. We don't brag about our country. We're typically modest and that's fine, but there is much to be proud of in this country.

Third, everybody counts. Every individual counts in our system of government—people who obey the law, people who are good citizens, those who are conscious of other people's rights, and those who are responsible. Everyone is important.

Even though I say I'm proud of what we have, that doesn't mean that we can't improve. Every individual should always try to improve our system of government.

Interviewers: How can children become involved in government?

Mr. Justice Iacobucci: I think there are a number of ways that children can be involved. They can visit government institutions, they can have guests come to their classes, such as representatives from the political parties or government or judicial institutions, and they can have projects of study.

They can participate in learning about and sharing experiences about those who are actively engaged in our government.

Interviewers: Thank you very much for your time today. We enjoyed meeting you.

Do Discuss Discover

1. Review the interview conducted with Justice Iacobucci. In your notebook, write a summary paragraph about what you learned from the interview.

Using Your Learning

Understanding Concepts

1. Make file cards for each of the Chapter 6 vocabulary words.
2. Complete the diagram of the structure of the federal government you began in Chapter 5. Add information about the Legislative and Judicial Branches. Remember, you may include pictures.

Developing Inquiry/Research and Communication Skills

3. Do research to identify the names of the current Supreme Court Judges.
4. What five questions would you like to ask your local MP about his/her role in government?

Applying Concepts and Skills in Various Contexts

5. In small groups, role-play the opening of Parliament or passing a bill into law.
6. Create a poster for recruiting students to be parliamentary pages.

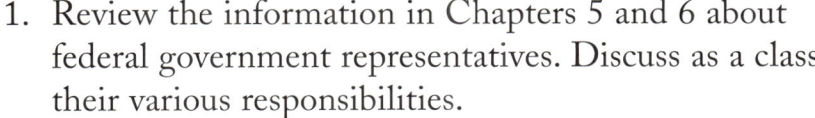

In Your Scrapbook

1. To learn about a federal government official, do one of these:

   a) Visit www.parl.gc.ca and click on "Senators and Members." List three current Senators and three current MPs. Try to include Senators and MPs from your area.

   b) Find a newspaper or magazine article about a Senator or MP.

2. Add your list or article to your scrapbook.
3. Complete an organizer. (See page 17.) Add it to your scrapbook.
4. Include your notebook copy of the House of Commons from the page 81 activity or another sample of your Chapter 6 work.

World Expo Link

1. Review the information in Chapters 5 and 6 about federal government representatives. Discuss as a class their various responsibilities.
2. With your project group, research a federal government representative.
3. Record the information in the chart you started in Chapter 4.
4. Share the responsibility within your group for writing a brief biography or summary about each person using information from the chart. Write each one on a file card.

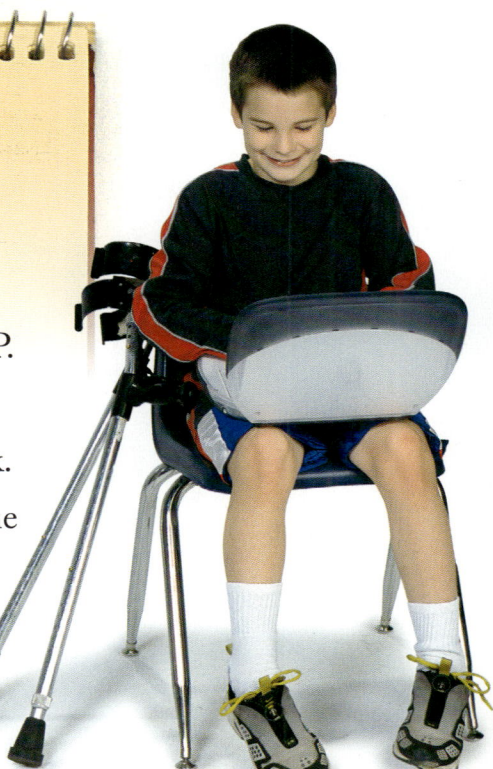

Chapter 7
Interactions Among Levels of Government

Necessary services and facilities in a community, such as roads, sewage systems, and hospitals, are its **infrastructure**. Infrastructure can be paid for by one, two, or all three levels of government. Sharing responsibilities can be complicated and challenging. It can also allow governments to meet the needs of citizens more efficiently.

" How can anyone not look at this and be excited about what we've achieved. This is a wonderful win for British Columbia, for Canada, and for Vancouver and Whistler. "

– Larry Campbell, Vancouver Mayor, upon the awarding of the 2010 Winter Olympics

Focus on Learning

In this chapter, you will learn about
- three levels of government working together in a crisis
- government in everyday life
- government interactions

Vocabulary
- infrastructure
- liaison

" It is with deep concern that we watch the on-going flood situation in Manitoba. Saskatchewan will provide whatever assistance Manitoba requires in the coming days and weeks. Again, let me say the thoughts of the people of Saskatchewan are with our neighbours in Manitoba during this time of need. "

– Roy Romanow, Premier of Saskatchewan in 1997

In a Crisis

When a crisis destroys people's homes and businesses and damages infrastructure, the community needs help from many sources. An example of such a crisis was the 1997 flood in Manitoba. Municipal, provincial, territorial, and federal governments worked together to help the community solve problems. There were also many volunteers and donations of money, clothing, food, and household goods from people across Canada.

When people, groups, and government services work together on a crisis, **liaison** is important. Liaison is the way that groups communicate and cooperate in challenges like the Manitoba flood crisis.

The Canadian Armed Forces and municipal crews work together during the Manitoba flood.

Soldiers and other citizens stack over 6.5 million sandbags along the river to protect property and buildings from the rising water.

Dear Carla,

I thought I should write to you before I collapse in my cot. I am sure you are watching the news. The pictures of the "Flood of the Century" cannot possibly show everything that is happening here. As you know, our home is close to the river, so we moved all the family albums, Mom's crystal, and our important papers to the attic for safekeeping.

Our school closed two days ago and everyone went home to help put sandbags around their homes. I never want to see another pile of sand in my life.

I may not get a chance to write to you for a couple of weeks since the army has moved us to the community centre. Before we left our home, Dad said we could each take one suitcase. I could hardly decide what to take! Now the army is patrolling our street so that the rest of our belongings will be safe.

This morning the Mayor declared a state of emergency and called for help from both the provincial and federal governments because the water continues to rise. At the centre, we heard from the Red Cross and volunteers that Canadians from across the country are helping in any way they can by sending clothing, blankets, medicine, food, and money.

My eyes are closing. I am going to end my letter now. I will try to write next week to fill you in on what is happening here.

Love,
Christina

Government in Everyday Life

Look at the scene on these two pages. Find as many examples of government interactions as you can. These could be interactions among levels of government or interactions between citizens and government. Use the outside border for clues. If you find 25, you are a super snoop!

Education
- universities
- schools
- daycares

Finances
- taxes
- Bank of Canada

Industry
- building permits
- factory regulations

Environment
- parks
- wardens
- fishing licences
- garbage removal
- regreening

Arts, Culture, and Heritage
- museums
- community centres
- libraries

Government Interactions

Form groups of four or five. Read the instructions below and follow the steps as outlined.

Instructions

1. In your small group, read the diary entry you have been assigned.
2. As a group, discuss and make a list of all the things, people, and services needed to successfully deal with the situation.
3. Create a T-chart organizer with the needs on one side and the level of government (municipal, provincial, and/or federal) responsible for those needs on the other Hint: Look at pages 47, 54, and 69 for help.

Example:

Needs	Level of Government
– a new hospital	– provincial

4. As a group, take the role of one level of government. Write a plan of action for how your level of government will deal with the scenario.

Around the World

By the time it is completed in 2009, the Three Gorges Dam in China will have taken 250 000 workers 17 years to build. All levels of government will be cooperating to complete this huge project. This includes finding new homes and farmlands for 1.2 million people. Eventually, the dam will produce one-ninth of all China's hydropower.

Dear Diary,

This is the fifth day of my quarantine. The local health officer has asked anyone who came into contact with a patient with SARS to be quarantined. It is very boring staying in my room now, although Mom and Dad moved the TV in here and bought many new books. I even get room service! There is good news—the government is going to help pay for Grandma to look after me when Mom goes back to work. On the news, Canada's Minister of Health was reporting to the World Health Organization, asking that Toronto's travel advisory be lifted. Each day, the newspapers discuss how restaurants and hotels are letting workers go because visitors are staying away from the city. Many concerts and conferences have been cancelled. Our Mayor, Premier, and Prime Minister are working hard to bring visitors back to Toronto now that SARS is under control.

Dear Diary,

What a thrill! I've got a job working at the Olympic site!

The city is expecting millions of people to begin pouring into our city within the next two months. There has been construction on all the major roads. Many new buildings, stadiums, and apartments have been built throughout the city. For the past year, travelling around the city has been next to impossible because of construction.

Last week, the Premier and Prime Minister met with the Mayor to lay the last cement tile on the entrance walkway. It has taken years for the city to prepare for this international event, and we are ahead of schedule!

Next week, I begin training for my job as a tour guide. I have already gone for my security clearance and photo ID. Safety and security for workers, athletes, and visitors are essential. RCMP officers are seen everywhere in the city, especially on the grounds. Their trained dogs continually search the area for sources of danger.

Dear Diary,

Last week, the national newspaper had a full-page article and advertisement calling for volunteer tree planters to repair last year's forest fire damage. My class is going to volunteer to work this Saturday. We talked in class about what happened in our community during the forest fire. Firefighters came from all around. Many local people went to help the army and firefighters as they battled the fire.

Private companies and the government will provide funding for the materials the volunteers will need to replant the forest. The seedlings that we will plant were grown in an underground mine in Sudbury! They must have used artificial light, I guess.

My aunt is looking forward to the volunteers who will come to her motel for food, refreshments, and a place to stay. The local stores are preparing for more business over the next few weeks, too. Our community will see new faces from all over the country.

Instant Orchestra

1. Collect items around the home, classroom, and schoolyard that can be used as musical instruments. Some examples are blades of tall grass, combs, small stones, a grater, tin cans, and glasses or bottles filled with water. If you do not have an instrument, you can make sounds to imitate one.

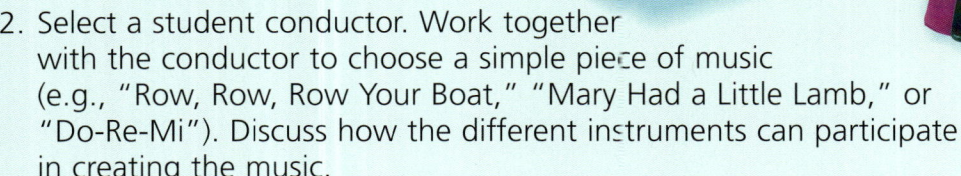

2. Select a student conductor. Work together with the conductor to choose a simple piece of music (e.g., "Row, Row, Row Your Boat," "Mary Had a Little Lamb," or "Do-Re-Mi"). Discuss how the different instruments can participate in creating the music.

3. The conductor divides the class into orchestra sections and practises the tune with each section.

4. Each section practises some more on its own. Once everyone knows the tune, the conductor brings the orchestra together to perform.

5. Give your performance.

6. Write a personal reflection about the following questions:
    a) What is the difference between the tune played by an individual, by one section, and by the whole orchestra?
    b) How is this like the three levels of government working together?

Using Your Learning

Understanding Concepts

1. Make file cards for each of the Chapter 7 vocabulary words.

Developing Inquiry/Research and Communication Skills

2. Explore www.winter2010.com to learn about the involvement of the three levels of government in the Vancouver/Whistler Olympic Games. Create an organizer showing the involvement of each level.

3. Choose one of the diary entries on pages 94 and 95. Write a reflection commenting on the responses of the three levels of government.

Applying Concepts and Skills in Various Contexts

4. In small groups, create a tableau that shows government interaction in one of the scenarios covered in this chapter.

5. Review the banana split graphic on page 45. Design a new graphic showing the three levels of government in Canada.

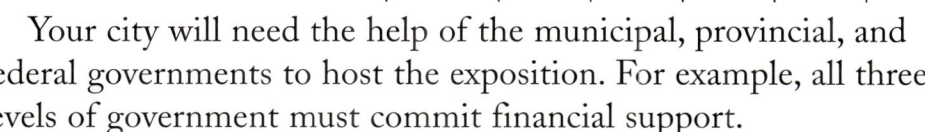

In Your Scrapbook

1. Do either a) or b) to learn about interactions among levels of government:

    a) Watch a television newscast. Write notes about one story.

    b) Find an article in a local or national newspaper.

2. Add your notes or the article to your scrapbook.

3. Complete an organizer. (See page 17.) Add it to your scrapbook.

4. Include your personal reflection from the activity on page 96 or another sample of your Chapter 7 work.

World Expo Link

Your city will need the help of the municipal, provincial, and federal governments to host the exposition. For example, all three levels of government must commit financial support.

1. As a class, recall your Chapter 4 predictions about the roles of the municipal and provincial governments in the exposition. Now discuss the role of the federal government.

2. In your project group, design an organizer showing your city's needs for the exposition and the level(s) of government that will help meet each need (e.g., services, facilities, and funding).

Chapter 8
Structures and Symbols

Words like "country" and "government" represent complicated ideas. These are not concrete objects that can easily be shown in a picture. Symbols are objects and images that represent important ideas. When we see the Parliament buildings, we know they stand for our federal government. We know our flag represents Canada.

"Good morning and welcome to our national capital, Ottawa. This is the home of our federal government. You have studied how our federal government works and takes care of Canadians. Now, let's tour some of Ottawa's important government buildings. We will see some of the symbols that decorate the buildings and also study some of the early parliamentarians connected with the buildings."

– Tana Godbout, tour guide, Ottawa, Ontario

Focus on Learning

In this chapter, you will learn about
- the buildings and symbols of Parliament Hill
- early Canadian parliamentarians
- the Canadian Coat of Arms
- the Supreme Court
- Rideau Hall

Vocabulary
- Eternal Flame
- Parliament Hill
- Centre Block
- Library of Parliament
- Peace Tower
- East Block
- West Block
- Rideau Hall

"Canadians have many different cultural origins, beliefs, traditions, and languages. Yet one flag—the Canadian flag—flies for all Canadians. Our flag symbolizes the unity of Canadian citizens and the strength that comes from our unity. I'm proud of our flag and our country."

– Vincent Yu, Halifax, Nova Scotia

Parliament Hill

As you walk toward the home of our parliamentary system of government, you will see a fountain. At the centre is the **Eternal Flame**, which burns continuously. Around the fountain are the shields of the Canadian provinces and territories. The water and flame represent Canada's unity from coast to coast. Coins tossed into the fountain by visitors go into a fund to help Canadians with disabilities.

There are three main buildings on **Parliament Hill**: the Centre Block, East Block, and West Block. The Supreme Court is nearby, west of the Hill. Around the grounds are statues of the Fathers of Confederation, members of royalty, former Prime Ministers, and other Canadians who made important contributions to our government.

On January 1, 1967, Prime Minister Lester B. Pearson lit the Eternal Flame to begin Canada's Centennial celebrations. That's why it is sometimes called the Centennial Flame.

The grounds of Parliament Hill are used during Canada Day celebrations, the changing of the Guards, and many concerts.

The Canadian Flag

The *Maple Leaf* became our official flag when it was adopted by the Parliament in 1964 and proclaimed into law by Queen Elizabeth II on February 15, 1965. At noon that day, the Canadian flag was raised on Parliament Hill in the presence of Governor General Georges Vanier, Prime Minister Lester B. Pearson, Members of Parliament, and thousands of Canadians. Red and white have been Canada's national colours since 1921. The maple leaf is a recognized Canadian symbol.

View from Above

Canada's federal government is located in Ottawa, Ontario, Canada's capital city. The Parliament buildings sit on the hill overlooking the Ottawa River, directly across from Gatineau, Quebec.

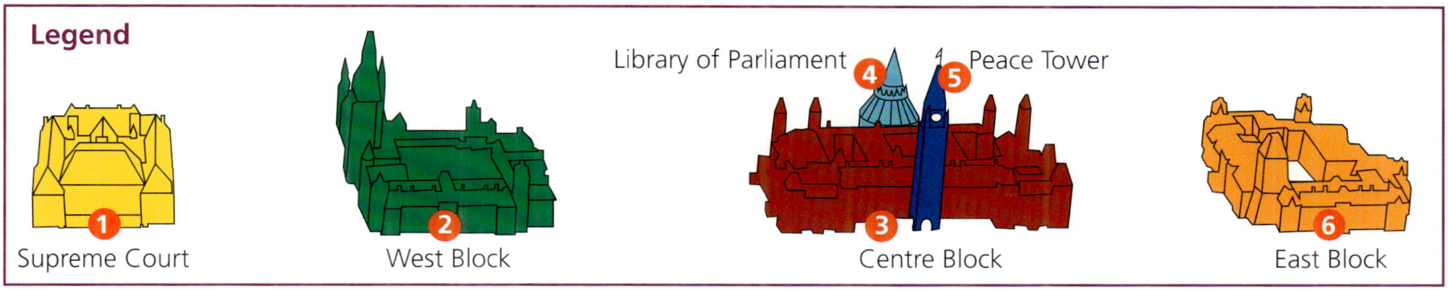

Legend

1 Supreme Court

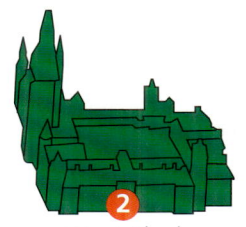
2 West Block

Library of Parliament 4   5 Peace Tower
3 Centre Block

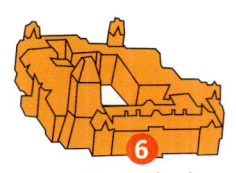
6 East Block

http://www.parliamenthill.gc.ca

Visit this website and click on "Explore the Hill" to take a virtual tour of Parliament Hill.

101

The Centre Block

The **Centre Block** contains several important parts of Parliament Hill. They are the House of Commons, the Senate, the Library of Parliament, and the Peace Tower.

House of Commons

The House of Commons occupies the western half of the Centre Block. The Chamber is decorated in green like the British House of Commons. Much of our parliamentary tradition comes from England.

This large room was built from Canadian white oak and Tyndall limestone from Manitoba. The ceiling is covered with Irish linen that was hand painted after it was installed. Around the room are stained glass windows illustrating the provincial and territorial flowers. One set of sculptures shows symbols of the parts of Canada's Constitution.

When Parliament is in session, Members of Parliament meet in the House of Commons. Visitors can watch from viewing areas called public galleries.

History and Art

The architects of Parliament Hill made sure that the paintings, sculptures, and carvings, such as the one on the right, would reflect Canada's Aboriginal, French, English, and immigrant roots. A sculpture of Tadadaho, shown below, is found in the House of Commons hall. Tadadaho was the head chief of the Ononadaga. He was the final chief brought into the Iroquois Confederacy, or League of Five Nations, the governing body of the Iroquois.

Early Members of Parliament

Canada has had a wealth of parliamentarians since it became a country. These are only a few of the many who could be highlighted.

Sir George-Étienne Cartier, 1814–1873

Sir George-Étienne Cartier is one of the Fathers of Confederation. He played a key role in forming the laws that have governed Canada. Cartier worked beside Sir John A. Macdonald as Minister of Militia and Defence. Queen Victoria knighted him in 1868 to recognize his contribution to Confederation. A statue of Cartier stands on the grounds of the Centre Block.

Agnes Macphail, 1890–1954

Agnes Macphail was born on a farm in Grey County, Ontario. Her interests in farmers' problems eventually led her into politics. In 1920, she became a Progressive Party candidate. This was unheard of! Many asked her to step aside to let a man take her place, but she refused. In 1921, she was elected in the constituency of Grey South East and became the first female Member of Parliament in Canada. She served as an MP for nearly 20 years.

Tommy (Thomas C.) Douglas, 1904–1986

As a boy, Tommy Douglas would have lost his leg to infection were it not for a doctor willing to treat him for free. He also lived through the hard economic times of the 1930s. His experiences inspired him to work for the well-being of others. He helped form what is now the New Democratic Party (NDP) and was elected MP in 1935. In 1944, he became Premier of Saskatchewan and 17 years later, federal leader of the NDP. By then, he had established Saskatchewan's health insurance plan, which included hospital and medical coverage. This paved the way for a nation-wide healthcare plan for all Canadians. Tommy Douglas, the "Father of Medicare," died in 1986, having served as a government representative for 44 years.

Do Discuss Discover

1. Write a personal reflection about the contributions that these early parliamentarians made to Canada.
2. a) Why do you think Agnes Macphail was asked to step aside and let a man replace her as a candidate?
   b) What would you have done?

The Senate

The Senate Chamber is situated on the east side of the Centre Block. Senators from every province and territory review bills passed in the House of Commons. They also introduce some bills of their own.

Two huge bronze chandeliers weighing over two tonnes each light the Senate Chamber. The upper walls are lined with eight large murals showing scenes of World War I. Flowers, creatures, and masks are carved on the white oak panelling all around the room.

The Senate has its own mace. This mace is a symbol of the Sovereign's command that the Senate meet to carry out the business of government.

The red carpeting and a gold ceiling have given this chamber its second name—the Red Chamber.

During sittings of the Senate, the mace rests on the table in front of the Speaker with its tip pointed toward the throne.

Cairine Reay Wilson, 1885–1962

Cairine Reay Wilson of Montreal was the first woman Senator in Canadian history. She was appointed to the Senate in 1930 and served until her death in 1962. She was also Canada's first woman delegate to the United Nations General Assembly.

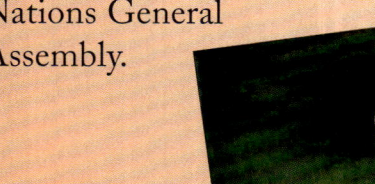

Charlie Watt, Senator

In the 1970s, Charlie Watt was a key negotiator for the Inuit. He helped reach a land-claim agreement called the James Bay and Northern Quebec Agreement. He also played a major role in writing Section 35 of Canada's Constitution that recognizes the rights of Aboriginal people. He helped start Inuit associations in Quebec and Air Inuit, Canada's first Aboriginal airline. He also promoted fisheries and Aboriginal businesses.

Charlie Watt was appointed to the Senate in 1984. He was made an Officer of the Order of Quebec in 1994 and received a National Aboriginal Achievement Award in 1997.

The Library of Parliament

The **Library of Parliament** is a magnificent building situated on the river side of the Centre Block. In this beautiful building, librarians gather information for Senators, Members of Parliament, staff, and members of the media.

Queen Victoria selected Ottawa as Canada's capital in 1857. She requested that a library be built to serve Parliament's needs for information, research, and documentation. The library was to bring together books and documents located in Toronto, Montreal, and Kingston.

The library was modelled after the Reading Room at the British Museum in London, England. It is shaped like a cone, with 16 flying buttresses supporting it. The building is topped with a copper roof. There are pinnacles, turrets, and elaborate iron works.

Thirty years after the library opened, the fire of 1916 destroyed the Centre Block. The stone and wooden entrance linking the library to the Hall of Honour had a set of very heavy iron doors behind the stained glass doors. When someone noticed smoke in the Reading Room, the iron doors were immediately closed. This act saved the library from the fire.

The iron structure of the library's dome was completely assembled in England and then shipped to Canada.

A white marble statue of Queen Victoria stands in the centre of the library's domed rotunda.

Michel Brisebois, Rare Book Curator, National Library of Canada

Michel Brisebois works at the National Library of Canada, another important library in Ottawa. He has a goal: to collect a copy of every Canadian book printed before Confederation. He is in charge of the rare book collection at the National Library of Canada. He has been dealing with books for more than a quarter century. He communicates on a daily basis with book dealers in Canada, the United States, England, and France. He feels that the collection of rare books is part of the heritage that belongs to all Canadian people.

The Peace Tower

The **Peace Tower** officially opened in 1928. The current 92.2 metre tower replaced the tower that was destroyed in the fire of 1916. It was originally built as a monument to the service and sacrifice of Canadian men and women during World War I. Over the years, it has come to symbolize Canada's commitment to world peace.

In 2000, a bill was introduced in Parliament to establish another Book of Remembrance for the men and women who died while on peacekeeping missions.

Over time, weather conditions and air pollution damaged the tower. A two-year project to secure the stones and clean lettering and sculptures was completed in 1996.

Nobel Peace Prize

In 1952, Lester B. Pearson was President of the United Nations General Assembly. He played an important role in developing the UN Peacekeeping initiative. His plan resulted in the peaceful resolution to the 1956 Suez Canal Crisis. In 1957, he was awarded the Nobel Peace Prize. In 1963, he became Canada's fourteenth Prime Minister.

An altar in the centre of the Memorial Chapel holds the World War I Book of Remembrance. Five other books list deaths in other conflicts. A page is turned every morning throughout the year.

Dear Grandma,

Today I climbed the many steps up to the Memorial Chapel in the Peace Tower. It is a beautiful room with stained glass windows. I was hoping to see Great-Granddad's name in the Book of Remembrance for the Battle of Vimy Ridge. It was sad to see how many people lost their lives.

Love,
Lana

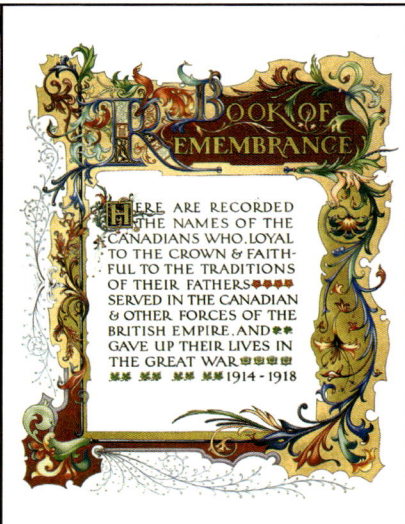

THE BOOK OF REMEMBRANCE

HERE ARE RECORDED THE NAMES OF THE CANADIANS WHO, LOYAL TO THE CROWN & FAITHFUL TO THE TRADITIONS OF THEIR FATHERS SERVED IN THE CANADIAN & OTHER FORCES OF THE BRITISH EMPIRE, AND GAVE UP THEIR LIVES IN THE GREAT WAR 1914-1918

The tower contains an observation deck, a memorial chapel, and the carillon. The 53 bells of the carillon are played from a large keyboard. Wires from the organ move the clappers that strike the bells. The outside of the tower is decorated with many sculptures. Each corner has a large stone carving of an unusual-looking creature. These are called gargoyles. There is also a large clock on each face of the tower.

Every summer day at 2:00 p.m., carillon music is played on Parliament Hill.

Dear Mom and Dad,

I heard the bells playing from the Peace Tower. They were very loud. I also had a chance to watch the carillonneur play the bells. He uses his fists and feet to make music. Maybe my piano playing will sound better if I use my fists. I'll try this when I come home.

Love,
Billy

The strange and scary faces of gargoyles are a type of traditional stonework found on many historic castles and public buildings in Europe.

Hey Joey,

Today I saw the ugliest statues in the world! Can you imagine that they did this on purpose? The tour guide at Parliament Hill said these statues were made to protect the buildings. When I design my next Halloween mask, I'm going to remember some of the faces on these guys.

See you soon.
Alex

Do Discuss Discover

1. Why is the Peace Tower one of the most recognizable symbols of Canadian government?
2. Why do you think the sculptors created gargoyles for this tower?

The East Block

The **East Block** was the centre of the Canadian government for the first 100 years. It was built to house the offices of the Governor General, Prime Minister, and Cabinet Ministers. Cabinet meetings were held there for more than 100 years. In 1910, this building also contained six massive vaults. These were originally used to store the nation's gold reserve. Today this gold is in the Mint.

The East Block now contains four restored historic rooms and the offices of current senators and MPs.

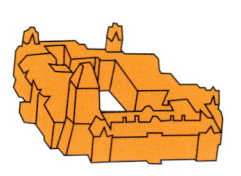

The copper roofs of the East Block and other Parliament Buildings were once copper-brown, but years of exposure to air and water causes copper to turn green.

Offices in the East Block have been re-created to look like they did at the time of Canada's Confederation.

Hi John,

Today we stepped back into time when we toured the office of Canada's first Prime Minister, Sir John A. Macdonald. The room has beautiful stained glass windows, a marble fireplace, gas lamps, and a cold-water basin. The Prime Minister even had a buzzer he could use to call his clerk (but no e-mail)!

Signing off,
Jack

Visitors to Parliament Hill can tour this restored office used by many of Canada's Prime Ministers, from Sir Wilfrid Laurier to Pierre Trudeau.

Hi Mavis,

Check out this office! It looks just like it did at the time of Sir George-Étienne Cartier. He served on Canada's first Cabinet. In his day, only Cabinet Ministers had offices. Members of Parliament had their desks in the House of Commons. I hope their desks were neater than mine at school!

Your pal,
James

Early Prime Ministers

There have been 20 Prime Ministers between 1867 and 2003. Some served for one term and others for several.

Sir John A. Macdonald, 1815–1891

As a child, John Alexander Macdonald immigrated to Kingston, Ontario, from Glasgow, Scotland. He grew up to be a persuasive speaker with great determination. He became a lawyer, entered municipal government as an alderman (councillor), and soon moved to provincial government. His skills as a politician helped to create the country of Canada.

On July 1, 1867, the Dominion of Canada was formed. Recognizing Macdonald's leadership, the people elected him as the first Prime Minister. Lord Monck, the first Governor General of the Dominion of Canada, swore him into office.

Macdonald worked long and hard shaping Canada as a country. He oversaw the West becoming part of Canada and encouraged settlement there. He encouraged British Columbia to join by promising a link to the east. That link became the Canadian Pacific Railway. Macdonald was knighted for his efforts in bringing about Confederation. He holds the title "Father of Confederation."

Sir Wilfrid Laurier, 1841–1919

Wilfrid Laurier was born in Saint Lin (Laurentides), Quebec. He became a lawyer and also a newspaper editor. He began his political career in 1871 as a member of Quebec's provincial legislature. He used his talents as a speaker to convince people of his viewpoints.

In 1896, Sir Wilfrid Laurier became Canada's first francophone Prime Minister. His long political career also included 30 years as an MP. Laurier believed maintaining national unity was his most important duty. He encouraged cooperation between French and English Canadians. He helped create the Yukon Territory, constructed a second transcontinental railroad, saw Saskatchewan and Alberta become provinces, and established the Royal Canadian Navy.

Laurier was knighted by Queen Victoria for his work in nation building. When he died in 1919, his huge state funeral was one of the first public events in Canada to be recorded on film.

The West Block

Originally, the East Block and **West Block** were to be the offices of all the ministers and federal civil servants. Today the West Block contains offices for MPs. Many of the rooms, such as those in the Laurier Tower and the Mackenzie Wing, are reminders of past leaders in Canadian government. The West Block is not open to the general public.

The West Block opened in 1866 and housed the Postmaster General and federal government departments. The Mackenzie Wing and Laurier Tower were added later.

The Confederation Room is one of the largest reception rooms on Parliament Hill. It is used for special occasions and conferences.

The Cat Sanctuary

Among the trees bordering the rear of Parliament Hill and near the statue of Queen Victoria is a small community of stray cats. There is a legend that these strays are descendants of the mousers that once roamed the corridors of The Hill in "Her Majesty's Service" when Victoria was Queen of England.

Since the late 1970s, the cat sanctuary has been home for over 20 cats. A volunteer, René Chartrand, has been looking after the cats for the past 12 years. He visits every day to feed and care for the cats. He builds them shelters out of plywood that he has modelled on the architecture of Parliament Hill.

Visitors to the cat sanctuary help with his work by donating funds for food, veterinary services, and supplies. Because he is getting older, René is looking for an assistant to give him a helping hand.

The Canadian Coat of Arms

Our Canadian Coat of Arms represents the heritage of our government and traditions.

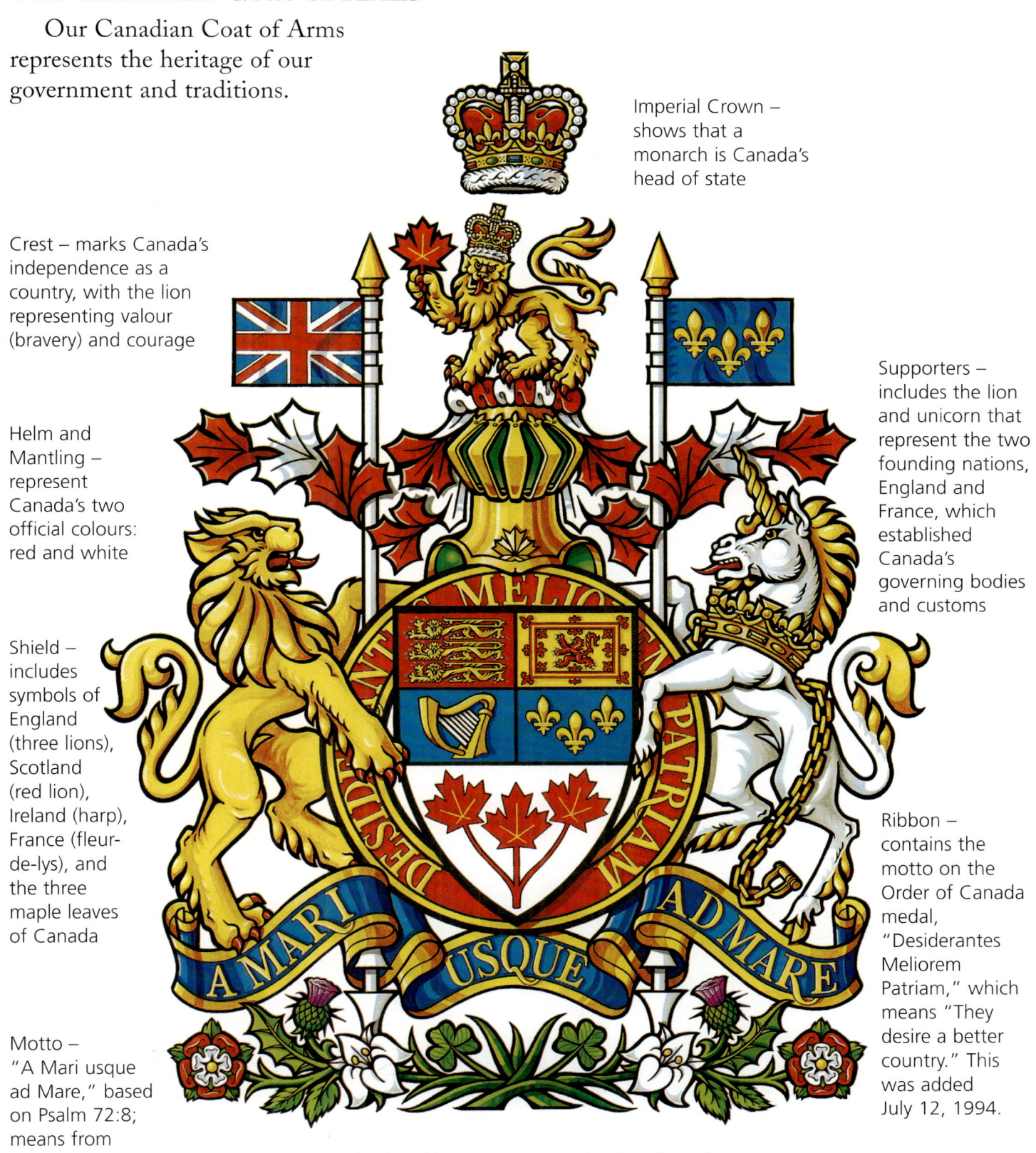

Imperial Crown – shows that a monarch is Canada's head of state

Crest – marks Canada's independence as a country, with the lion representing valour (bravery) and courage

Helm and Mantling – represent Canada's two official colours: red and white

Shield – includes symbols of England (three lions), Scotland (red lion), Ireland (harp), France (fleur-de-lys), and the three maple leaves of Canada

Motto – "A Mari usque ad Mare," based on Psalm 72:8; means from sea to sea

Supporters – includes the lion and unicorn that represent the two founding nations, England and France, which established Canada's governing bodies and customs

Ribbon – contains the motto on the Order of Canada medal, "Desiderantes Meliorem Patriam," which means "They desire a better country." This was added July 12, 1994.

Four Floral Emblems – represent the four founding nations: the English rose, the Scottish thistle, the Irish shamrock, and the French fleur-de-lys

The Supreme Court

West of Parliament Hill, on Wellington Street, stands a tall building set in a large park—the Supreme Court. When both flagpoles are flying the Canadian flag, the court is in session.

Ceremonial robes are on display in the Gallery off the entrance. They are red and are trimmed with Canadian white mink. They are only worn for special occasions such as the opening of a new session of Parliament.

The main courtroom has walnut panelling, large windows, and modern technology. The nine chairs for the judges sit at the front of the court. The Chief Justice of Canada sits in the centre of the row. The Canadian Coat of Arms looks down on the justices and the participants.

All court proceedings are televised. The courtroom has interpretation equipment. There is a special satellite link to allow lawyers in other provinces or remote areas to argue and listen to their case without coming to Ottawa. Directly behind the court is the Justices' Conference Room, which is lined with very old law books. Before they proceed into the court, the justices sit in this room at a round table to discuss the cases.

The private chambers of the nine justices and their private research library are on the second floor. The library is used by the justices and their laws clerks to research and prepare for cases.

The public can take guided tours or sit in on hearings in the Supreme Court to learn about Canada's justice system.

Walter S. Allward, a Toronto artist, created the two statues standing at the entrance to the Supreme Court of Canada.

Hi Tinesha,

While touring Ottawa today, I met Truth (Veritas) and Justice (Justitia)! Actually, they are two statues that greet judges, visitors, lawyers, and the media as they climb the steps to Canada's highest court. There is also a statue of former Prime Minister Louis St. Laurent on the front lawn. Pretty impressive!

Bye for now,
Tyler

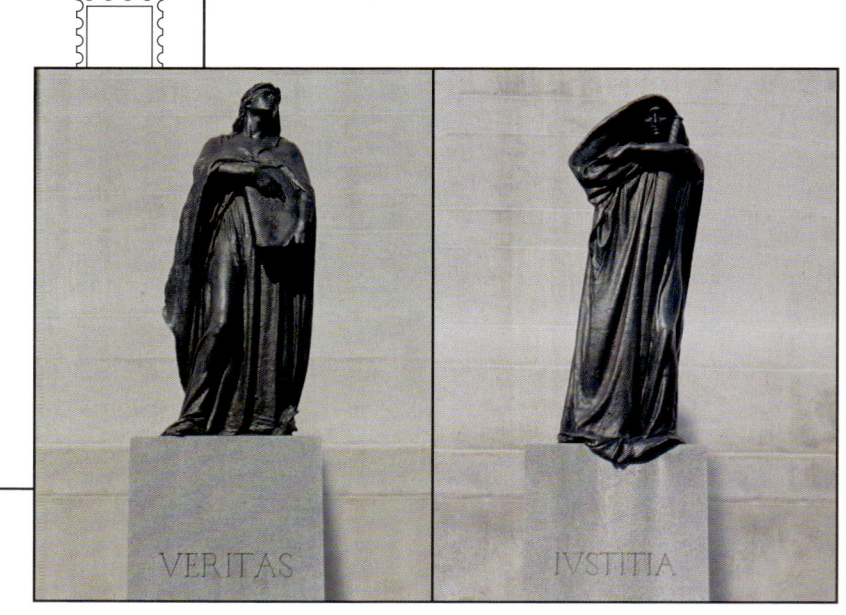

Building a Structure

You will need
- camera and film
- 3-D geometric solids
- geometric nets
- poster-paper
- pencils and scissors
- paints, pencil crayons, felt markers
- glue

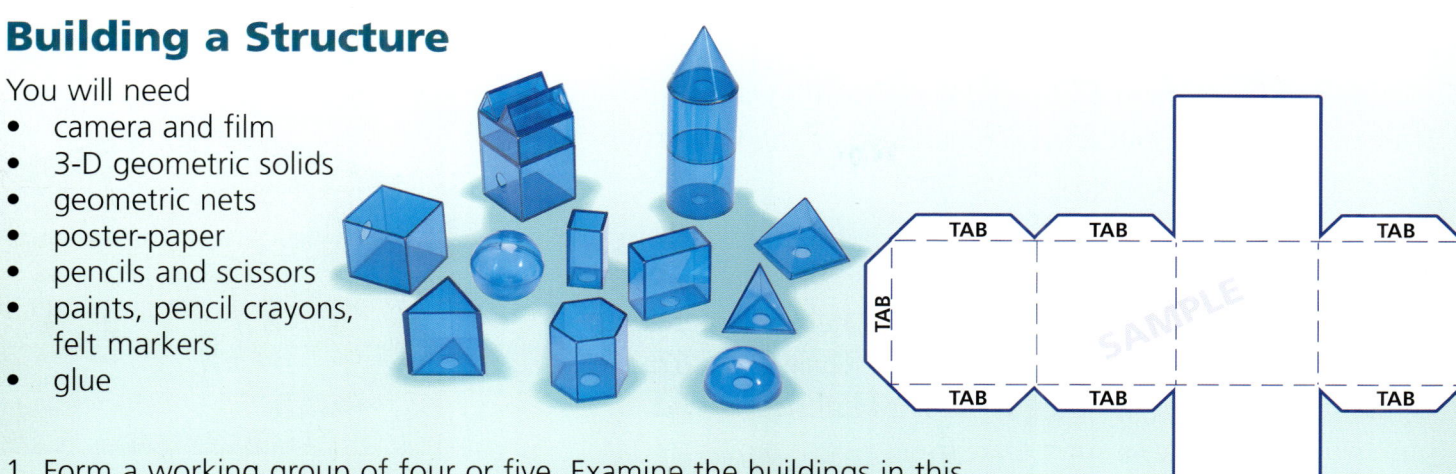

1. Form a working group of four or five. Examine the buildings in this chapter. Select a building for which you would like to create a model.
   - Centre Block
   - East Block
   - West Block
   - Library of Parliament
   - Supreme Court
   - Peace Tower
   - Rideau Hall (See page 114.)

2. Assign one group member to take pictures of the different stages of the creation of your structure. These photographs will be used later to create a photo essay.

3. Use the 3-D geometric solids to plan your model. Select the nets you will need to create your model.

4. Enlarge the nets as needed and carefully trace them onto poster paper.

5. Cut out your poster-paper nets.

6. Paint your nets. Use pencil crayons and markers to add details.

7. Assemble your nets by gluing the tabs together.

8. Create and decorate a base for your structure.

9. Arrange the photographs in chronological order on a display board or on poster paper. Create captions to accompany them.

Rideau Hall

On a quiet corner of Sussex Drive in Ottawa stands **Rideau Hall**. It is the Official Residence of the Governor General of Canada.

This residence had eleven rooms when it was built in 1838 for Thomas Mackay and his large family. Mackay named his house after the Rideau Canal, which he helped build. He also owned several mills on the Rideau River. In 1867, the Canadian government bought Rideau Hall. It has had numerous renovations since that time.

Today leaders and other important visitors from around the world stay at the Governor General's residence while visiting Ottawa.

Summer visitors to Rideau Hall can see the changing of the guard, called Relief of the Sentries, every hour.

Two sentries in ceremonial dress stand at attention at the entrance—perfectly still, rain or shine.

Woods, rich gardens, and lawns surround Rideau Hall. There are more than 10 000 trees on this property. More than 100 of the trees were planted by visiting royalty and world leaders. Families can visit the grounds and gardens of Rideau Hall, have a picnic, or see a totem pole and an inuksuk. In the winter, visitors can go skating on the outdoor skating rink.

The Tent Room is still used for formal receptions and dinners.

The house includes a ballroom, reception rooms, offices, a greenhouse, and fabulous antiques and artworks. In the Canadian Room, there is a collection of magnificent Canadian arts and crafts. One amazing room was added by Lord Dufferin as an indoor tennis court. It is called the Tent Room. To prepare it for gatherings, the walls were covered in red and white awning material.

In the Ballroom, the Governor General presents the honours and awards that celebrate Canadian excellence such as the Order of Canada, the Caring Canadian Award, and the Academic Medal.

24 Sussex Drive

Built in 1866, this limestone building was first the home of a lumber mill owner. He called it Gorffwysfa, which is a Welsh word meaning "place of peace." In 1951, 24 Sussex Drive became the official residence of Canada's Prime Ministers. Louis St. Laurent was the first to live there. The elegant building overlooks the Ottawa River.

Early Governors General

In 1952, the Right Honourable Vincent Massey became the first Canadian Governor General who had been born in Canada. Before that, they were sent from Britain. Anglophone and francophone appointments are usually alternated.

The Governor General is in residence at Rideau Hall if the Governor General's standard is flying outside it. The standard is a blue flag with a crowned gold lion holding a maple leaf.

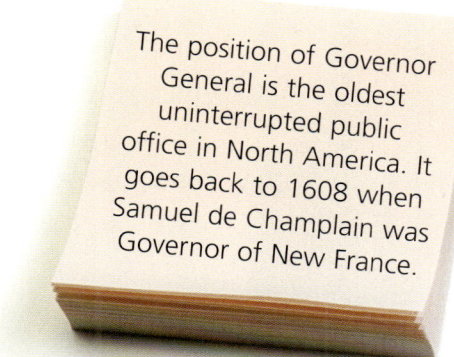

The position of Governor General is the oldest uninterrupted public office in North America. It goes back to 1608 when Samuel de Champlain was Governor of New France.

When the Governor General travels in Canada, this flag is flown from buildings that she or he visits.

The Right Honourable Vincent Massey encouraged achievements in the arts and other fields in order to build Canadian identity.

Canada's Governor General Lord Stanley donated the Stanley Cup in 1892. Governor General Earl Grey donated the Grey Cup in 1909.

Hi Anna,

I know you're a huge hockey and football fan, but did you know that the Stanley Cup and Grey Cup competitions were being played 100 years ago? I didn't! The University of Toronto won the first Grey Cup. The Montreal Amateur Athletic Association won the first Stanley Cup, but Lord Stanley was in England and missed it all. Thank goodness we have television!

Paul

Reflecting on Symbols

"Now we have finished our tour of Rideau Hall and Parliament Hill. Here are some symbols of Canada you have seen. What are some questions about these symbols you would like to ask?"

Why is the Speaker's Chair placed on a raised platform?

Why would they use a weapon to represent the power of Parliament?

Why is it important that each country have symbols to represent it?

Why does this flag include a lion?

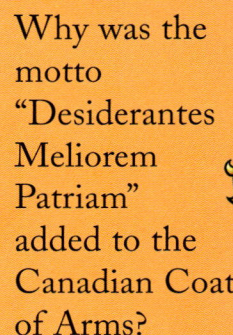

Why was the motto "Desiderantes Meliorem Patriam" added to the Canadian Coat of Arms?

Why does this statue have its eyes closed?

Around the World

A flag is an important symbol of a country. The flag of Nigeria was first raised on October 1, 1960. On that date, Nigerians celebrated becoming independent from Britain. The flag's green panels represent agriculture. The white panel stands for peace and unity.

Do Discuss Discover

1. With a partner, discuss your answers to the questions above. Identify three other symbols of Canada. What do they represent?

Using Your Learning

Understanding Concepts

1. Make file cards for each of the Chapter 8 vocabulary words. Include architectural words also found in this chapter.

2. Create an organizer about the government buildings described in this chapter. Include the type of building, the year it was built, its purpose, and an interesting fact.

Developing Inquiry/Research and Communication Skills

3. Choose an early parliamentarian and create a timeline of important events in his or her life.

4. Write a letter that might be included in a Book of Remembrance for Canadian peacekeepers, to thank them for their sacrifices.

Applying Concepts and Skills in Various Contexts

5. Create a *Heritage Moment* about an important event or person in Canada's government.

6. In small groups, create a presentation that a tour guide might use to showcase one of the buildings included in this chapter.

In Your Scrapbook

1. Obtain a postcard, a picture from a travel brochure, or a newspaper article about a government building or Canadian symbol.

2. Add it to your scrapbook.

3. Complete an organizer. (See page 17.) Add it to your scrapbook.

4. Include your personal reflection from DDD question 1 on page 103 or another sample of your Chapter 8 work.

World Expo Link

1. As a class, discuss symbols that could be displayed at the exposition to represent the three levels of government.

2. With your project group, create a small poster for each level of government. Use pictures and symbols, but not words, to represent each level.

3. In Chapter 9, your group will be creating a model of Canada's exposition pavilion. Individually, create a detailed sketch. Consider your exposition theme as you plan. Make notes and sketches of possible decorations and signs for the outside of the building.

Chapter 9
Federal Elections

A free election is an important right in all democratic countries. The citizens vote to choose members of their government. The **electoral process** includes all the steps taken to choose a government.

"The right to vote is the very basis of our system. It is given to every citizen in recognition of his or her intrinsic worth as a human being. It is a fundamental principal of a democracy and it is recognized by the Canadian Charter of Rights and Freedoms."

– *Jean-Pierre Kingsley, Chief Electoral Officer of Canada*

Focus on Learning

In this chapter, you will learn about
- how federal governments are elected in Canada
- the political and organizational parts of elections
- writing a speech
- elections and the media
- election day
- how the government is formed

Vocabulary
- electoral process
- campaign
- nomination
- platform
- polling station
- majority government
- minority government
- Official Opposition
- by-election

A sculpture called *The Vote* is found on the east wall of the House of Commons chamber. It is a large wheel with an "X" in the centre to symbolize the mark voters make on their ballots. The stone at its base, shown above, shows four heads whose singing mouths shape the first syllables of Canada's national anthem, "O-Ca-na-da." Their faces stand for all people in Canada who have the right to vote.

The Electoral Process

In Canada, a federal election must be held within five years of the previous election. The Prime Minister decides when it is needed. At that time, he or she meets with the Governor General to request that Parliament be dissolved, or closed, and to announce the election date.

There are two parts to every electoral process: the political part and the organizational part. The candidates, who want to be elected as Members of Parliament, participate in the political part of the process.

People who work for Elections Canada provide the organizational part.

The Electoral Process

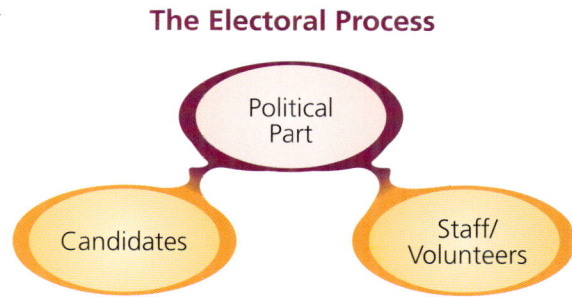

Elections Canada

Federal elections are organized by an impartial agency called Elections Canada. The Chief Electoral Officer is its head. Elections Canada is not connected with any political party and does not support any candidates. The Chief Electoral Officer is appointed by, and reports directly to, the whole House of Commons. The Chief Electoral Officer is one of the few people not allowed to vote in an election because he or she needs to be impartial.

Elections Canada is responsible for making sure elections are held fairly. These people make it easier for citizens to vote, but they do not tell them who to vote for.

The Electoral Process

Around the World

China is a communist country. Its main party is the Chinese Communist Party or CCP. There are also eight small registered parties that are controlled by the CCP. Candidates need the approval of the Chinese Communist Party in order to run. No parties other than the CCP and the eight smaller parties were allowed to run during the October 2002 to March 2003 elections.

Sheila Copps, Minister of Canadian Heritage, participates in the electoral process by casting her vote in Hamilton, Ontario.

The Political Part of the Process

Candidates take part in the political part of the electoral process. Candidates are women and men from all walks of life who want to be elected to Parliament. They spend a lot of time and effort making their ideas and those of their political party known to the voters, especially during an election **campaign**. A campaign is an organized series of activities that leads to election day.

In a federal election, any Canadian citizen who is 18 or older can become a candidate, with a few exceptions. Senators, members of provincial and territorial legislatures, some judges, prisoners, the Chief Electoral Officer, and the many other election officers cannot run for election.

Political Parties

Most candidates belong to political parties. Political parties are made up of people who share similar ideas about the roles and responsibilities of government.

There are usually more than ten registered federal political parties. The following are the five federal political parties with seats in Parliament:

Jack Layton, Leader of the NDP Party, looks for public support in an upcoming election.

Peter MacKay, Leader of the PC Party, joins a campaign rally. These are commonly held during an election period.

Political Party	Logo	Leader (2003)
Bloc Québécois		Gilles Duceppe
Canadian Alliance		Stephen Harper
Liberal Party of Canada		Jean Chrétien
New Democratic Party (NDP)		Jack Layton
Progressive Conservative Party of Canada (PC Party)		Peter MacKay

Campaigning for Election

In most ridings, each political party chooses one candidate to represent their policies and ideas. The party holds a **nomination** meeting to decide who to name as their candidate in the riding. A riding is an electoral district. Riding means the same as constituency.

Candidates set up a campaign headquarters to coordinate their election campaign. Usually, a campaign manager and a financial manager are paid workers. The rest of the people working in the office are usually volunteers.

The road to victory for candidates is hard work. For at least 36 days, they travel throughout their riding trying to meet as many voters as possible. They make speeches at various community functions. They knock on the doors of homes and try to convince voters to give them their support. The purpose of the campaign is to make the candidate well known to the voters in the electoral district.

A few candidates do not belong to political parties. They campaign as independent candidates. If they are elected, they sit in Parliament as independent MPs.

Party Leaders' Campaigns

The national leaders of the main parties are often busier than most candidates. They campaign in their own riding like other candidates, but they also travel to every region in the country. They represent their political party and work to convince voters in the country to select candidates from that party.

Party leaders take part in debates seen on national television, visit radio stations, speak at campaign rallies, and try to have newspapers write positive articles about their party's **platform**. A party's platform is the members' set of beliefs about issues and their plans for changes.

Party leaders also want Canadians to be familiar with their names and pictures because they all hope to become the next Prime Minister of Canada.

Gilles Duceppe, Leader of the Bloc Québécois, shows support for one of his party's candidates during an election campaign.

Volunteers from each party post signs in public areas encouraging voters to choose their candidate.

Persuasive Writing: Writing a Speech

A speech is a type of **persuasive writing**. We give speeches to persuade others to look at issues and topics from our point of view. A good speech must be entertaining, informative, and influential. That means it should influence or change what the listener thinks or will do.

Parts of a Speech

- an interesting opening
- a main idea
- facts to back up your main idea
- strong closing statement

1. Decide what you will speak about and create an outline.

2. Write your speech. Begin by stating the main idea so the listener immediately knows your purpose.

3. In the body of the speech, aim to convince the audience to agree with your opinion. Choose your main points. Under each main point, include facts and solid reasons that support the main point. Mention the opposite viewpoint and show its weakness.

4. Write a strong closing statement by summarizing your most important points.

5. Re-read your speech. Check that you used language that will interest listeners and encourage them to understand and agree with your message. Consider adding personal stories and props. Make changes as needed.

6. Slowly read your draft out loud to see how long it is. Either add to it or condense it to fit the time requirements.

7. Write brief point-form notes about your main points on cue cards. Practise saying your speech until it is familiar to you and you can say it smoothly using your cue cards.

Do Discuss Discover

1. Write a speech about an issue that is important to you or your school; for example, longer physical education classes or more books in the library.

Elections and the Media

Candidates and leaders of political parties want voters to remember them and their ideas. They rely on the media to relay their points of view and party platforms to voters. The way politicians present themselves and the way the media presents them is called their image. For example, they usually want to be seen by voters as trustworthy, intelligent, and interesting.

Reporters

Most major newspapers and radio and television networks assign reporters to follow the party leaders as they travel across the country from riding to riding.

Each day, reporters write about what the leaders do and say and about the audience they have been addressing. They also report on the issues being debated during the election. Local newspapers in the ridings often present feature pages on each candidate and his or her stand on the election issues.

Reporters depend on Elections Canada to provide them with background information on the election process and maps of the ridings. Some regulations affect what the media can report. For example, on election day, no riding results can be given out until all the voting locations have closed.

Federal party leaders present their party's position on important issues and challenge each other's ideas during debates.

Many candidates have websites. Government, media, and Elections Canada websites are also sources of election information.

Candidates try to reach as many communities as possible during a campaign. Many party leaders, such as former Prime Minister Joe Clark, have a campaign bus.

Around the World

Australia has a democratic system of government. Voters select members to the House of Representatives. Voting by all citizens is required in both the federal and state elections. Citizens who do not vote in an election may be fined.

Do Discuss Discover

1. As a class, discuss why riding results cannot be broadcast until all voting locations have closed.

Being an Informed Citizen

It is the responsibility of citizens to gather as much information as possible on the issues and the candidates. Voters (electors) are responsible for making an effort to find the candidate and party that best fit their hopes for their community and Canada.

Voters can research election issues by watching debates between party leaders on national television. They can also listen to the radio, read newspapers and magazines, and search the Internet.

"Because we have a right to vote, we have a responsibility to properly prepare for the election. If we research all the candidates, we can make an informed decision. We can listen to the radio, read the newspapers, watch TV, read the candidates' pamphlets, attend candidates' meetings, and talk about the issues with our friends and family. It takes time and effort to choose a candidate with good ideas who will do the best job of representing our interests."

– *Sam Harrison, Timmins, Ontario*

"I volunteered to help my local candidate. Election campaigns are costly and time consuming. Volunteers help by mailing letters, fund-raising, answering phones, putting up lawn signs, handing out pamphlets, and driving seniors to the polling stations. I've learned so much about politics, government, and being a responsible citizen— and I've experienced the excitement of an election firsthand!"

– *Janice Lowry, Moncton, New Brunswick*

"After we become adults at 18, we have the right to vote for a person to represent our ideas and interests in Ottawa. The candidate with the most votes in our riding becomes our MP. The MP must represent all the people in the riding, whether or not they voted for him or her."

– *David Neville, Regina, Saskatchewan*

Do Discuss Discover

1. Make a checklist that a citizen could follow to prepare to vote under the following categories: What should I know? What should I do?

The Organizational Part of the Process

The Member of Parliament for each electoral district or riding represents about the same number of people. From time to time, riding boundaries are changed when there are increases or decreases in population. In 1997, the number of ridings in Canada was increased from 295 to 301. It is expected that by 2004 there will be 308 seats.

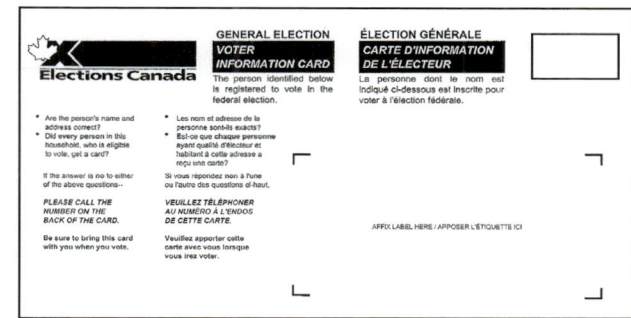

Before a federal election, all eligible citizens receive a Voter Information Card. It tells the address and hours of operation of the polling station where voters will mark their ballots.

Duties of Elections Canada

- make sure laws about elections are followed
- maintain the National Register of Electors, a computer database of the names of all Canadians who are eligible to vote
- train election officers, including the returning officers who supervise the election in each riding
- set up voting places, called **polling stations**, in the community. Most polling stations are located in school auditoriums and community centres.
- prepare the ballots in each riding, placing the candidates' names in alphabetical order
- make recommendations to Parliament to improve the election process
- provide support when changes are made to riding boundaries

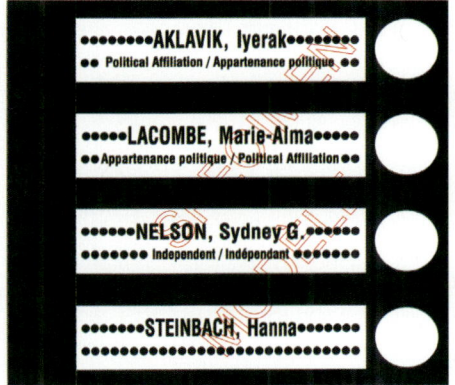

Election officers check their lists to find each voter's name as she/he arrives. Each name is crossed off to prevent anyone from voting twice.

Do Discuss Discover

1. Why do you think the candidates' names are in alphabetical order on the ballot?
2. After reviewing the duties of Elections Canada, why do you think this group is important to the election process?

Election Day

1. Take your Voter Information Card to the polling station.

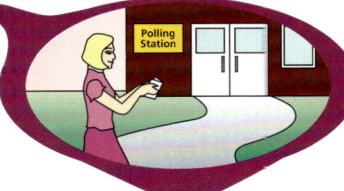

2. At the polling station, locate the numbered ballot box that matches the number on your Voter Information Card.

3. Give your card to the election officer at that ballot box. He or she will find your name on the voters' list, and then cross it off the list to show that you have come to vote.

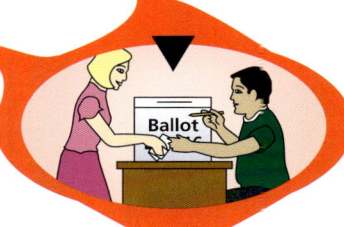

4. The Deputy Returning Officer (DRO) will give you a folded ballot.

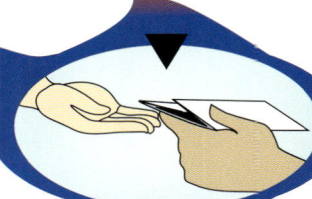

5. Take your folded ballot behind a voting screen. The screen is there to make sure your vote is secret.

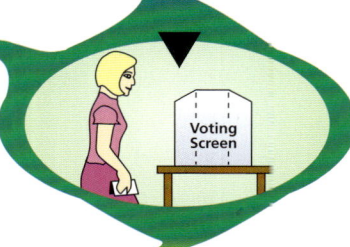

6. Open the ballot. It lists, in alphabetical order, the names of all the candidates running in your riding.

7. Find the candidate of your choice. Mark an "X" in the circle beside the candidate's name. The "X" is your vote.

8. Fold the ballot again to make sure your vote remains secret.

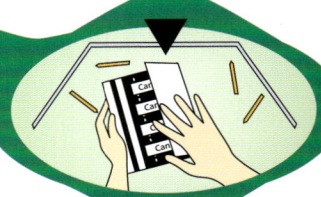

9. Return your ballot to the DRO.

10. The DRO will tear off the tab without opening the ballot and return the ballot to you.

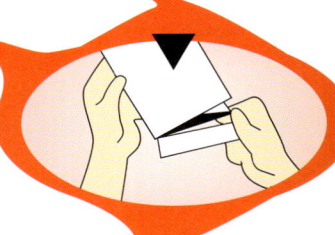

11. Place the vote into the ballot box.

12. Return home to watch the news on television, check the Internet, or listen to the radio for reports of results.

Forming a Government

After the election, the successful candidate in each riding becomes its Member of Parliament. The party with the largest number of elected members forms the government, and its leader becomes the Prime Minister.

If a party's candidates win in 151 or more of the 301 ridings, it will form a **majority government**. In Parliament, all of a party's members are usually expected to vote the same way on important bills. Having a majority government makes it easier to make laws.

If the winning party has fewer than 151 seats, it will form a **minority government**. In order to make laws, a minority government needs to get support from MPs from other parties.

The party that has the second-highest number of seats in the House of Commons is called the **Official Opposition**. The role of the Official Opposition is to ask questions and challenge the government about issues and decisions.

All MPs, both opposition and government, are expected to represent the interests of their consituencies as well as follow the platforms of their political parties.

By-elections

Sometimes MPs resign because of illness or personal reasons. Whenever a seat becomes vacant, a **by-election** is held to fill it. This is an election in a single riding.

During the years between federal elections, there may be several by-elections. Sometimes a candidate from another party will be elected in a by-election. This changes the number of seats held by the government or the opposition parties.

Stephen Harper leads the Canadian Alliance and is the Leader of the Official Opposition in the House of Commons.

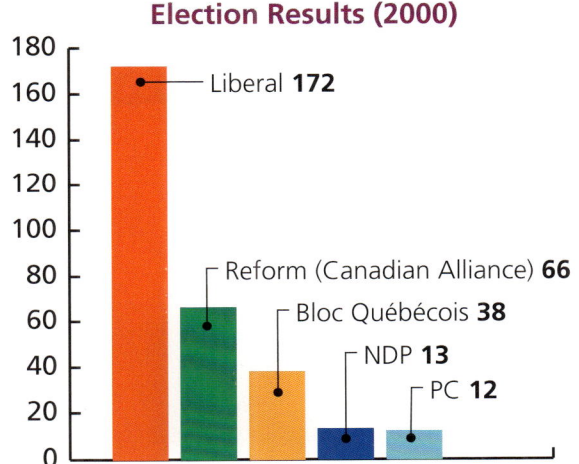

Election Results (2000)
- Liberal 172
- Reform (Canadian Alliance) 66
- Bloc Québécois 38
- NDP 13
- PC 12

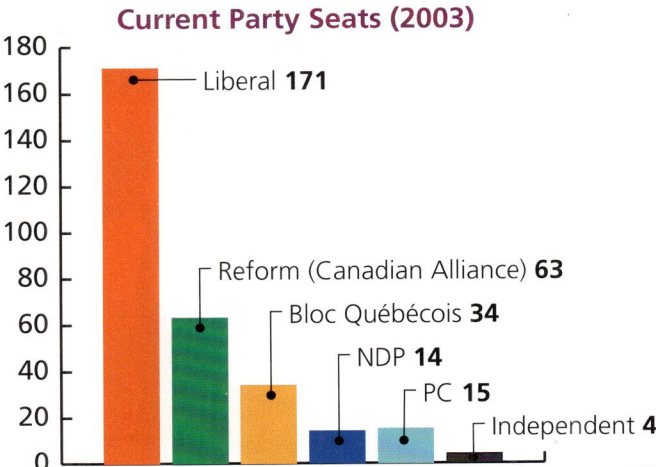

Current Party Seats (2003)
- Liberal 171
- Reform (Canadian Alliance) 63
- Bloc Québécois 34
- NDP 14
- PC 15
- Independent 4

Do Discuss Discover

1. Review page 36 about reading statistics. Discuss, in groups, the two graphs on this page. Which party formed the majority government? Which is the Official Opposition? Write two statements in your notebook about the changes from 2000 to 2003.

Election Game

DIRECTIONS: Play in groups of three or four "candidates." Take turns flipping a coin to move your marker forward.
Heads = 2 spaces
Tails = 1 space
When you land on a step, read it aloud, and then follow the direction in parentheses.

Your family and friends encourage you to run for office.
(+1 space)

Your local MP is retiring and asks you to run in his/her place in the constituency.
(+2 spaces)

START!

You want to stand as an independent candidate.
(Wait here a turn)

Deposits and signatures are not submitted in time, three weeks before Election Day.
(Out of the game)

You find a campaign headquarters and hire a campaign manager.
(+2 spaces)

You deposit $1000 to the government and get signatures of 100 or more qualified electors in the riding.
(+2 spaces)

The local newspaper misquotes you and mixes up the names on the photograph.
(−2 spaces)

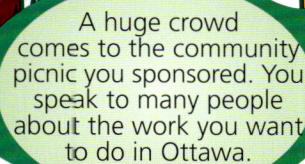

A huge crowd comes to the community picnic you sponsored. You speak to many people about the work you want to do in Ottawa.
(+2 spaces)

You present your party's platform on the issues at the all-candidates meeting.
(+1 space)

Your signs on the main street are all taken down. The volunteers need to replace them.
(−2 spaces)

Election Simulation

In this simulation, you can personally experience the hard work and excitement of candidates and volunteers in a federal election as well as that of Elections Canada workers.

1. Discuss selecting a student parliament for your classroom with your teacher. Brainstorm issues that could be resolved by a student parliament. Decide on issues candidates might present to the voting students.

2. Divide the class into five groups. Four of the groups will represent political parties, and the fifth group will represent Elections Canada.

Elections Canada Group

This group is responsible for

- listing the eligible voters
- creating the ballots
- setting up the polling station
- notifying voters of their polling station
- preparing signs to encourage voters to vote
- handing out the ballots
- counting the ballot results
- recording the results
- notifying all candidates of the election results.

Four Political Party Groups

These groups are responsible for

- selecting a party name and logo
- selecting a candidate
- preparing posters, buttons, and campaign literature
- helping the candidate campaign
- preparing a speech dealing with the issues that their candidate will give at an all-candidates meeting (See page 122.)
- preparing announcements about their party and the election
- stopping the campaigning on the day of the election.

Using Your Learning

Understanding Concepts

1. Make file cards for each of the Chapter 9 vocabulary words.
2. In your notebook, locate the chart you created for the DDD on page 5. Make additions and changes. Add it to your scrapbook.

Developing Inquiry/Research and Communication Skills

3. Visit www.elections.ca. Click on "Past Elections" and then "Voter Turnout at Federal Elections and Referendums" to find out the percentage of voters who participated in the last federal election.
4. Write a persuasive paragraph encouraging citizens to exercise their right to vote.

Developing Map/Globe Skills

5. Sketch riding boundaries on a regional map. Include the riding names, and highlight the riding in which your school is located.

Applying Concepts and Skills in Various Contexts

6. Using an organizer like the one on page 13, compare Canada's type of government with another type of government in the world.

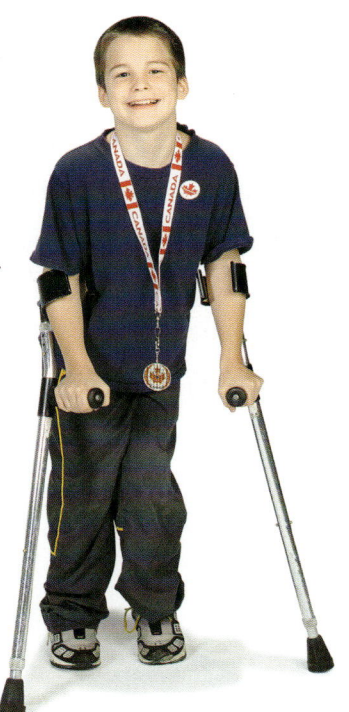

In Your Scrapbook

1. If there is an election happening in your area, obtain a campaign pamphlet, OR if there is no election happening, locate a newspaper article that deals with a current issue in Canada.
2. Add the pamphlet or article to your scrapbook.
3. Complete an organizer. (See page 17.) Add it to your scrapbook.
4. Include your speech from the DDD on page 122 or another sample of your Chapter 9 work.

World Expo Link

You have been learning about the rights and responsibilities of the different participants in the electoral process. You have also participated as a member of your project group.

1. Work with your group to review your pavilion sketches. Decide together which one best represents your theme or use ideas from each.
2. Collect the materials needed to create your pavilion. Decorate and colour it. For example, add symbols and signs to the outside.
3. Together, write an explanation of the meaning of the design.

Finishing Touches

In Your Scrapbook

1. Create a title page to glue on the front of your scrapbook. Include your name and the beginning and end dates of your entries, and add a picture about your study of *Faces of Government*.

2. Check that you have written the chapter title and number at the beginning of each chapter section.

3. Check that you have included all required articles and notes, as well as the chart from Using Your Learning question 2 on page 131.

4. Make sure organizers for each chapter are included and complete.

5. Check that you have included a sample of your work for each chapter.

The Exposition Display

Creating a Diorama

In your project groups, plan and create a diorama of the inside of your pavilion by completing these steps:

1. Keeping your theme in mind, plan and sketch a basic design for your diorama structure. Consider using a large box or three-sided display board.

2. Highlight the three faces of government you researched. For example, use small dolls or drawn cut-outs as models for each person. Place them inside the display near the summary or biography cards you created in Chapter 6.

3. Add symbols and other decorations to the inside of the pavilion.

Organizing Your Display

1. Working with your project group, gather the various parts of the project you completed. This could include the pavilion model, diorama, promotional poster, organizer showing needs and levels of government, and three small posters representing each level of government. Plan to include your scrapbooks, as well.

2. Decide together how you will organize the items to create your World Exposition display.

Personal Reflection

1. In your group, write down ten important things you learned about government. Use your scrapbook and notebook for ideas.

2. In your group, discuss how you could become more involved in government at the community level.

3. After the group discussion, write a personal reflection of what government means to you. Include your plans for involvement as a responsible citizen in the government process.

4. Share your draft personal reflection with your group. Ask them for editing suggestions.

5. Polish your draft.

6. Prepare to present your individual reflections to the visitors at your display.

Sharing Your Work

1. In the gym or library, work with your group to arrange your scrapbooks and exposition display.

2. Invite other classes, parents, and teachers to view your display and hear your personal reflections.

Glossary

A

affirmation—the act of declaring agreement with something, such as the rights and responsibilities of citizenship

ambassador—the head of an embassy that represents Canada in another country

amendment—a change to a written statement

appeal—a request to have a higher court review and rule upon a decision made by a lower court

B

bill—a suggested law before it is passed by a provincial, territorial, or federal legislature

by-election—an election held in the time between elections to fill an empty seat with an elected representative

bylaw—a local law approved by a majority of councillors in a municipality

C

Cabinet—MPs chosen by the Prime Minister and appointed by the Governor General to deal with important issues and head government departments; in provincial/territorial governments, the Premier selects from elected members, except in Nunavut, where MLAs select from among themselves

Cabinet Minister—an MP (or MPP, MLA, MNA) selected from elected members to deal with issues of importance in Canada and head a government department; *see also* Cabinet

campaign—the organized activities of a candidate intended to convince citizens to vote for her/him to be their elected representative

Canadian Charter of Rights and Freedoms—a document that lists the legal rights of Canadian citizens

Canadian Coat of Arms—an image that represents Canada's heritage and traditions in symbols

candidate—a person who chooses to run for an elected position in government

Centre Block—a building on Parliament Hill that contains the House of Commons, the Senate Chamber, the Library of Parliament, and the Peace Tower

Chief Electoral Officer—the impartial head of Elections Canada responsible for making sure elections are held fairly

citizen—a person who lives in a municipality, province or territory, and country

citizenship—having the standing of a citizen with all the rights, privileges, freedoms, and duties of a citizen

civil servant—a non-elected person who works for any level of government; examples are deputy ministers, senior officials, scientists researchers

civil service—the permanent, non-elected workers in government who carry out the laws, rules, and work of government

Confederation—the union of provinces and territories to create Canada; in 1867, Ontario, Quebec, Nova Scotia, and New Brunswick were the first to join

consensus—a decision-making process in which all the participants come to an agreement about a choice or an issue

constituency—a riding or electoral district with an elected federal, provincial, or territorial government representative

constitution—a written set of rules explaining how a country will be governed

councillor—an elected member of a municipal government

D

democracy—a system of government in which citizens of the country elect representatives to make laws and decisions based on the needs and wishes of the people

dictatorship—a system of government in which the leader makes all the laws and decisions

diplomat—someone who represents Canada in negotiations with other countries

E

East Block—a building on Parliament Hill that historically contained the offices of the Governor General, Prime Minister, Cabinet Ministers, and several vaults that held Canada's treasures

election—choosing government representatives by voting

electoral district—a riding or constituency with an elected federal or provincial government representative

electoral process—the steps followed to choose a new government

embassy—a building and group of people, including an ambassador, that represent Canada in another country

Eternal Flame—continuously burning flame found in the fountain at the entrance to Parliament Hill; the water and the flame represent Canadian unity

F

federal government—the central government of Canada that creates and enforces laws and runs programs for all of Canada; a system of government in which power is divided between the country's central government and a number of provincial or territorial governments

G

government—a group of people who provide leadership and organization, make decisions and laws, and enforce laws to meet the needs of its citizens

Governor General—an appointed representative of the Sovereign in Canada; mainly a ceremonial role

H

head of state—the monarch or leader of a country; the British monarch has a ceremonial role as Canada's formal head of state

House of Commons—the group of elected Members of Parliament (MPs) responsible for debating important issues and making laws; also refers to the room where MPs meet on Parliament Hill in Ottawa

I

immigrant—a person who freely moves to another country intending to live there

impartial—not taking either side in an issue or decision; fair

independent candidate—someone who is running for election to government without connection to or the backing from a political party

independent judiciary—a branch of government that discusses, interprets, and rules on laws without the influence of the rest of government

infrastructure—services and facilities that meet the needs of communities, such as transportation, power, and water systems

J

judiciary—the courts and judges who form an independent branch of government that interprets and enforces laws

L

landed immigrant—a person who has moved from another country and is living as a legal resident in Canada

law—a federal bill passed by the House of Commons and Senate and signed by the Governor General; in provincial or territorial governments, a bill passed by members of the Legislative Assembly and signed by the Lieutenant-Governor or Commissioner

Legislative Assembly—the branch of provincial and territorial governments made up of elected representatives responsible for discussing issues and making laws

liaison—communication between groups that enables them to work together

Library of Parliament—a building on Parliament Hill where books and documents are kept and librarians gather information for government representatives, staff, and the media

Lieutenant-Governor—the representative of the Sovereign in a province; appointed by the Governor General on the advice of the Premier

local government—municipal government; government of a town, village, county, city, district, or other nearby community area

M

majority government—a government formed by a political party that wins in more than half of the ridings

mayor—leader of government for an urban municipality such as a city

Member of Parliament (MP)—an elected representative who debates issues and makes laws in the House of Commons

minority government—a government formed by a political party that has gained fewer than half of the ridings in an election; it needs the support of representatives from other political parties to pass bills

monarchy—a system of government led by a king, queen, or emperor who inherits the position; today, most also have an elected parliament

multicultural—having citizens from many parts of the world who are encouraged to maintain and share their culture, customs, and beliefs

municipal government—government of a town, village, county, city, district, or other local community; also called local government

municipality—an urban or rural area defined by a boundary and governed by a council

N

naturalized citizen—an immigrant who has participated in the affirmation ceremony and has legally become a Canadian citizen

nomination—a meeting held to choose a candidate in a riding to represent a political party's policies and ideas

O

Official Opposition—the political party that wins the second-largest number of ridings during an election and holds the second-largest number of seats in the House of Commons

P

Parliament—a group of elected representatives who make laws for their country; also the place where they meet

Parliament Hill—the location of Canada's federal government in Ottawa; includes the Centre, West, and East Blocks

pavilion—a structure built at an exposition site to hold a country's displays and exhibits

Peace Tower—part of the Centre Block on Parliament Hill built as a monument to Canadian service men and women of World War I; now a symbol of Canada's dedication to world peace

platform—a political party's set of beliefs about issues and their plans for changes

political party—a group of people who share the same ideas about what their elected representatives should do for their nation, province, or territory

polling station—a place in the community where citizens go to record their vote

Premier—the elected leader of a provincial or territorial government

Prime Minister—the elected leader of a federal government; leader of the political party with the most elected MPs

R

reeve—the elected head of a rural municipal government such as a town council

refugee—someone who leaves one country and goes to another for safety and security

responsibility—a duty expected of the citizens of a country to make sure everyone's rights are respected and needs are met

Rideau Hall—the official residence of the Governor General of Canada, located in Ottawa

riding—a constituency or electoral district with an elected federal or provincial government representative

right—a privilege or freedom passed as law by a government for the good of its citizens

Royal Assent—the signing of a bill by the Governor General representing the Sovereign to make it law

Royal Canadian Mounted Police (RCMP)—the federal police department; also provides police services to all provinces, the territories, and several municipalities

S

self-government—Aboriginal-controlled government responsible for decision making, laws, and services instead of being part of a municipal, provincial, or territorial government

Senate—part of Parliament made up of appointed government representatives who participate in law-making

Senator—a person appointed by the Governor General to the Senate on the recommendation of the Prime Minister; examines issues of importance to Canadians and can introduce, change, or reject bills

Speaker of the House—a Member of Parliament elected by the MPs to make sure the rules and traditions of Parliament are followed; a Speaker is also chosen by Senators for the Senate

Supreme Court—part of the Judicial Branch of the federal government and Canada's highest court; its nine judges, appointed by the Governor General, interpret and rule on legal matters for all of Canada

T

Throne Speech—a speech written by the Prime Minister and read by the Governor General at the opening of Parliament stating the government's plans

V

volunteer—someone who freely gives her or his time and effort to benefit others in the community; the action of freely giving one's time and effort

W

ward—a municipal division or area with one or more elected representatives

West Block—a building on Parliament Hill that houses the offices of MPs

World Exposition—a fair where many countries display their achievements

Index

A
Aboriginal nations 14, 56-57, 59, 66, 84, 102
Aboriginal self-government 56, 57
Act
  Act of Parliament (1875) 86
  British North America (BNA) Act 21
  Citizenship Act 19, 38
  Constitution Act (1982) 21
  Municipal Act 50
  Species at Risk Act 85
affirmation 38-39. See also Oath of Citizenship, reaffirmation ceremony
Allward, Walter S. 112
Amagoalik, John 57
ambassador 74
amendment 21
ancient Greece 14
appeal 86
armed forces 5, 19, 45, 65, 91, 109
Around the World 25, 37, 53, 65, 86, 94, 116, 119, 123
Australia 123
awards 26, 64, 104, 106. See also Governor General Awards

B
ballot 125, 126
Band Council 56
bill 55, 77, 84, 85, 104, 106
Book of Remembrance 106
branches of government 52, 53, 62, 63, 64, 68, 76, 77, 86
by-election 127
bylaw 50

C
Cabinet. See also Cabinet Minister
  federal 63, 68, 108
  provincial/territorial 52, 53, 57
Cabinet Minister 63, 68, 76, 108, 110. See also Ministries
campaign 11, 120, 121, 123, 124
Canada Pavilion 6-7
Canadian Charter of Rights and Freedoms 21, 22-23, 38, 118
Canadian Citizenship Act 19
Canadian Coat of Arms 20, 111, 112, 116
Canadian flag 2, 3, 20, 98, 99, 112, 116
candidate 55, 103, 119, 120, 121, 123, 124, 125, 126, 127
Caribana Festival 41
carillon 107
Castro, Fidel 13
cat sanctuary 110
celebration 38-39, 41, 57, 65, 99
Centre Block 99, 101, 102-107
Chief Electoral Officer of Canada 119, 120
  Jean-Pierre Kingsley 3, 118
Chief Justice of Canada 21, 112. See also Supreme Court
Chile 37
China 94, 119
citizen 4, 5, 18-26, 30, 34, 37, 38-39, 40, 41, 55, 88, 120, 124. See also citizenship
Citizen Stamp 19
citizenship 2, 18, 19, 25, 30, 31, 32, 34, 37, 41. See also Citizenship Affirmation Ceremony, Oath of Citizenship, reaffirmation ceremony
Citizenship Affirmation Ceremony 38-39. See also reaffirmation ceremony
Citizenship Week 19
civil servants 70. See also armed forces, Chief Electoral Officer, civil service, Elections Canada, RCMP
  aquatic coordinator, facilitator 58
  Canadian diplomat 74
  clerk of the court 38, 39
  foreign service officer 71
  intergovernmental affairs specialist 59
  legislative page 59
  park warden 71
  parliamentary page 80
  presiding officer 38, 39, 40
  rare book curator 105
  RCMP blacksmith 73
  whale researcher 71
civil service 62, 63, 70. See also civil servants, services
Clarkson, Adrienne. See Governor General
Commander in Chief 64
Commissioner 53, 55, 57
Confederation 19, 63, 66, 99, 103, 108, 109
Confederation Room 110
consensus 14
constituency 77, 82. See also electoral district, riding
constitution 21, 86, 102, 104
council 46, 47, 49, 50
councillor 46, 49, 50
  Bussin, Sandra 49
Cuba 13

D
democracy 2, 10, 13, 14, 22, 62, 86, 118
Deputy Returning Officer 126
dictatorship 13
diplomat 74
dissolving Parliament 64, 119

E
East Block 99, 101, 108, 110
election 5, 21, 22, 118, 123
  federal 118-130
  municipal 11, 49
  provincial/territorial 53, 55, 57
Elections Canada 119, 123, 125
electoral district 77, 125. See also constituency, riding
electoral process 118-121, 123-127
embassy 74
Eternal Flame 3, 99
Executive Branch 52, 53, 62-74

F
federal government 44, 45, 54, 56, 62-74, 76-80, 82, 84-88, 91, 100
funding 45, 46, 47, 54, 69

G
gargoyle 107
government 3, 4, 5, 8, 56, 92-93, 98, 127
government interactions. See interactions
Governor General 63, 64, 65, 68, 78, 79, 84, 85, 86, 108, 114-115, 116, 119. See also Governor General Awards
  Clarkson, Adrienne 2, 5, 37, 64, 65, 67
  Dufferin, Lord 67, 114
  Grey, Earl 115
  Massey, Vincent 115
  Monck, Lord 109
  Stanley, Lord 115
  Vanier, Georges 99

Governor General Awards 64
   Academic Medal 67, 114
   Caring Canadian Award 67, 114
   Meritorious Service Decoration 67
   Order of Canada 66, 74, 111, 114
   Order of Merit of the Police Services 67
   Peacekeeping Service Medal 72
group needs 4-5

H

Hands On
   Building a Structure 113
   Creating a Class Canadian Flag 9
   Designing a T-Shirt for Volunteers 27
   Governing Bodies 15
   Instant Orchestra 96
   Making a Citizenship Banner 35
   Making a Mural 81
   Making a Shopping Bag Ad 48
Head of State 64, 111
House of Commons 63, 68, 76, 77, 78-79, 80, 82, 84, 85, 102, 104, 118, 119, 127. See also Parliament

I

immigrant 19, 30, 31, 32, 33, 36, 38. See also landed immigrant
impartial 77, 119
In Your Scrapbook 8, 17, 29, 43, 61, 75, 89, 97, 117, 131, 132
independent candidate 121
independent judiciary 86
infrastructure 90, 91
interactions 90, 92-93, 94-95
Israel 25

J

Jamieson, Roberta 56
judges 38, 86, 112 See also Chief Justice of Canada
   Cruden, Ruth 30
   Iacobucci, Mr. Justice (Honourable) Frank 76, 87-88
   McLachlin, Right Honourable Beverley 21
   Roberti, Roberto 30
Judicial Branch 21, 22, 52, 53, 63, 76, 86-88, 112. See also judges, Supreme Court
Justice (statue of Justitia) 112

K

King Bhumibol Adulyadej of Thailand 12
King Fahd bin Abd al-Aziz Al Saud of Saudi Arabia 12

L

landed immigrant 31, 32, 34, 37
Laurier Tower 110
laws 4, 19, 45, 50, 53, 55, 56, 63, 72, 76, 77, 84, 85, 86, 87
Leader of the Official Opposition 76, 78
Legislative Assembly 52, 53, 55, 57, 59. See also Member of Provincial Parliament (MPP)
Legislative Branch 52, 63, 76-80, 82, 84, 85. See also Legislative Assembly, House of Commons, Parliament, Senate
Legislature. See Legislative Assembly
levels of government 44, 45
Lewis, Stephen 74
liaison 91
Library of Parliament 101, 102, 105
Liechtenstein 65
Lieutenant-Governor 52, 53, 55
   Bartleman, James K. 53
local government 45. See also municipal government

M

mace 78, 79, 104, 116
Mackenzie Wing 110
majority government 127
Manitoba flood 90, 91
map 32
mayor 11, 46, 49
   Campbell, Larry 90
   Lastman, Mel 46
   McCallion, Hazel 44
media 11, 38, 78, 105, 121, 123, 124, 126
Member of Parliament (MP) 57, 63, 68, 77, 80, 85, 102, 108, 110, 124, 127. See also party leader, Prime Minister
   Adams, Peter 82
   Augustine, Jean 3
   Cartier, Sir George-Étienne 103, 108
   Copps, Sheila 119
   Douglas, Tommy (Thomas C.) 103
   Ittinuar, Peter 57
   Macphail, Agnes 103
   Martin, Paul, Jr. 14
   Martin, Paul, Sr. 19
   McClelland, Anne 76
   Pettigrew, Pierre 68
Member of Provincial Parliament (MPP) 52, 53, 55
Memorial Chapel 106, 107
Ministries 52, 58, 63. See also Cabinet, Cabinet Minister, services
minority government 127
monarchy 12, 21, 111. See also Queen Elizabeth II, Queen Victoria
municipal government 44, 45, 46-47, 49, 50, 91
municipality 46, 47, 49, 50
multicultural 30, 31, 33, 41, 84

N

National Library of Canada 105
National Register of Electors 125
naturalized citizen 38
New Zealand 13
Nigeria 116
Nobel Peace Prize 106
nomination 121
Nunavut 44, 53, 57, 65

O

O Canada 20, 40, 118
Oath of Citizenship 30, 34, 38-39, 40
Official Opposition 76, 127
opening of Parliament 64, 78-79
opposition parties 82, 127. See also Official Opposition
Order of Canada. See Governor General Awards
Ottawa 7, 63, 67, 82, 86, 98, 100, 105, 114

P

page 3, 59, 78, 80
Parliament 12, 19, 63, 64, 65, 68, 72, 77, 78-79, 84, 86, 102, 105, 106, 116, 119, 120, 125, 127. See also House of Commons, Member of Parliament, Parliament Hill/Buildings, Senate
Parliament Hill/Buildings 3, 20, 63, 98-108, 110, 112

party leader 63, 103, 120, 121, 123, 127. *See also* Prime Minister
   Chrétien, Jean 62, 68, 120
   Duceppe, Gilles 120, 121
   Harper, Stephen 76, 120, 127
   Layton, Jack 120
   MacKay, Peter 120
Peace Tower 3, 101, 102, 106-107
Pericles of Athens 10
platform 121
poem 23, 26, 59,
political party 55, 63, 120, 121, 123, 127. *See also* party leaders
polling station 125, 126
Pope John Paul II 20
Premier 52, 53, 55, 57, 68
   Charest, Jean 2
   Douglas, Tommy (Thomas C.) 103
   Okalik, Paul 44
   Romanow, Roy 90
Presiding Officer 38, 39, 40
Prime Minister 63, 68, 74, 78, 79, 84, 86, 99, 108, 109, 114, 119, 121, 127
   Campbell, Kim 2, 62
   Chrétien, Jean 62, 68, 120
   Clark, Helen (of New Zealand) 13
   Clark, Joe 123
   King, Mackenzie 19, 110
   Laurier, Sir Wilfrid 108, 109, 110
   Macdonald, Sir John A. 103, 108, 109
   Pearson, Lester B. 6, 99, 106
   St. Laurent, Louis 114
   Trudeau, Pierre 21, 108
Prince Hans Adam II 65
programs 33, 45, 56, 68, 70
provincial government 44, 45, 50, 52, 53, 54, 91

Q
Queen Elizabeth II 21, 39, 41, 53, 64, 65, 99
Queen's Park 52, 59
Queen Victoria 103, 105, 109, 110

R
reaffirmation ceremony 40. *See also* Citizenship Affirmation Ceremony
Red Chamber 104
Red Cross 91
reeve 46
   Rigney, Ross 49
refugee 31, 71
responsibility 4, 5, 18, 21, 25, 45, 50, 63, 77, 88, 90, 119, 120, 124
Rideau Hall 114
riding 55, 63, 77, 123, 124, 125, 127. *See also* constituency, electoral district
right 4, 5, 20, 21, 22-23, 24, 88
Royal Assent 64, 85
Royal Canadian Mounted Police (RCMP) 5, 20, 39, 72, 73

S
Saudi Arabia 12
scrapbook. *See* In Your Scrapbook
Senate 76, 78, 79, 84, 85, 102, 104
Senator 78, 84
   Chalifoux, Thelma 84
   Watt, Charlie 104
   Wilson, Cairine Reay 104
Sergeant-at-Arms 78, 79, 82
services 33, 48, 50, 90, 92-93. *See also* civil service, civil servants
   Aboriginal self-government 56
   federal government 68, 69, 70
   municipal government 47
   Ontario provincial government 54
Skill Pages
   Asking Questions to Gather Information 51
   Getting Information from Quotations 11
   Interviewing 83
   Persuasive Writing: Writing a Speech 122
   Reading Statistics and Drawing Conclusions 36
Sovereign 52, 63, 64, 104. *See also* monarchy, Queen Elizabeth II, Queen Victoria
Speaker of the House 77, 78, 79, 80, 82, 116
   Milliken, Peter 77
Speaker's Chair 79, 116
Speaker's Mace. *See* mace
Spirit of Canada (coin) 41
statistics 31, 32, 36, 37, 77, 84, 127
structure of government 46, 52, 63
structures (government buildings) 52, 53, 74, 78-79, 86, 112, 113, 114. *See also* Canada Pavilion, Parliament Hill/Buildings
Supreme Court 63, 76, 86, 87-88, 99, 100-101, 112. *See also* Chief Justice of Canada
Switzerland 53
symbols 3, 20, 63, 72, 78, 79, 98, 99, 102, 111, 116

T
Tadadaho 102
Tent Room 114
territorial government 44, 45, 52, 53, 57
Thailand 12
Throne Speech 37, 64, 65, 79
Truth (statue of Veritas) 112, 116
types of governments 10, 12-14, 15

U
United Nations 20, 24, 74, 104, 106
United States 74, 86
   Cohen, William S. 12

V
volunteer 26, 33, 49, 58, 59, 67, 91, 110, 121, 124
Vote, The (sculpture) 118
Voter Information Card 125, 126

W
ward 49
websites 28, 29, 42, 50, 60, 65, 72, 89, 97, 101, 131
West Block 99, 101, 110
World Expo Link 7, 29, 43, 61, 75, 89, 97, 117, 131, 132-133
World Expositions 6-7

Y
Yellowknife, NT 52

The World